Creative Styles of Preaching

Creative Styles
of Preaching

Mark Barger Elliott

Westminster John Knox Press
Louisville, Kentucky

Scripture quotations from the New Revised Standard Version of the Bible are copyright © 1989 by the Division of Christian Education of the National Council of the Churches of Christ in the U.S.A. and are used by permission.

Book design by Sharon Adams
Cover design by Night & Day Design

First edition

Published by Westminster John Knox Press
Louisville, Kentucky

This book is printed on acid-free paper that meets the American National Standards Institute Z39.48 Standard. ∞

PRINTED IN THE UNITED STATES OF AMERICA

The Fred Craddock sermon "When the Roll Is Called Down Here" is from Joseph Webb, *Comedy in Preaching* (St. Louis: Chalice Press, 1998) and is reproduced by permission of Chalice Press.

The Barbara Brown Taylor sermon "God's Daring Plan" is copyright 1997 by Barbara Brown Taylor. All rights reserved. Reprinted from *Bread of Angels,* which is available from Cowley Publications, 28 Temple Place, Boston, MA 02111; www.cowley.org (1-800-225-1534).

The Samuel Proctor sermon "On Giving Up on People Too Soon" is from *Sermons from the Black Pulpit* by Samuel D. Proctor and William D. Watley, © 1984 by Judson Press, Valley Forge, PA. *Sermons from the Black Pulpit* is available through Judson Press, 1-800-458-3766.

The Leonora Tubbs Tisdale sermon "The Gospel We Don't Want to Hear (or Preach)" is from *Journal for Preachers,* Easter 2000, and reproduced by permission.

Library of Congress Cataloging-in-Publication Data is on file at the Library of Congress, Washington, D.C.

ISBN 0-664-22296-X

For Lynn, Brendan, and Auden

Contents

Preface

*M*ost congregations quickly attune themselves to a particular style of preaching.

After only a few sermons, they anticipate when we will tell a joke or muse on current affairs. They note what magazine subscriptions we keep, what types of movies we take in on a Saturday night, and if we garden or play golf. They know exactly when a sermon is finished, even before we turn the last page.

The relationship between pastor and congregation can soon resemble a family reunion: the same folks show up and share the same stories.

Many of our church members, however, live in a world of compact disc players that shuffle ten discs, remote controls that herd five hundred channels, and Wal-Marts with the square footage of a small county. Church members have grown accustomed to and even *demand* variety. My wife admits she no longer can listen to just one compact disc. At the grocery store, I expect wines from Chile, Australia, and South Africa.

The humble premise of this book is that our congregations have grown, or will soon grow, restless with one preaching style. To keep their attention, pastors need to learn how to "shuffle," to arrive at our Sunday morning reunion with a greater variety of styles and yarns to share.

Consider *Creative Styles of Preaching* as a travel guide of the homiletical landscape. Here you will find nine sermon styles described in broad brush strokes and two sermons as examples for each style. My hope is that one (or more) will catch your fancy and encourage an extended stay.

Acknowledgments

As a runner who draws strength from whistles and a timely cup of water along the way, I'd like to thank and express gratitude to the many people who encouraged this project across the finish line.

For my wife and family, who were willing to grant me the gift of time. Thanks to my parents and sister who taught me the love of language and a good book. I am also grateful to Tom Long, whose passion for preaching was contagious.

Special thanks to the administrative staff of First Presbyterian Church, Ann Arbor, who retyped many of the sermons. And, finally, without the generosity of the wonderful folks who contributed these sermons, this project would never have found its stride. Thank you.

Mark Barger Elliott
Ann Arbor, Michigan
January 2000

Chapter 1

Narrative Preaching

If we were pressed to say what Christian faith and life are, we could
hardly do better than hearing, and living a story. *And if asked for a*
short definition of preaching could we do better than shared story?
Morris J. Niedenthal and Charles L. Rice[1]

Introduction

*C*harles Campbell places the origin of narrative preaching with H.
Grady Davis, who wrote in 1958 that "we preachers forget that the
gospel itself is for the most part a simple narrative of persons, places,
happenings, and conversation."[2] In the past forty years, homileticians
including Fred Craddock, Edmund Steimle, and Eugene Lowry have
absorbed Davis's observation and fashioned what is called "narrative
preaching," a style that recognizes the power of stories to shape and
nurture our faith.

But even after forty years, confusion still exists as to what classi-
fies a sermon as "narrative." Is it a twenty-minute story that alludes
to a scripture text? A loosely connected series of illustrations that
relate to one another like reports on the evening news? A first-
person sermon with costume and headdress? In his essay, "Narrative
and Preaching: Sorting It Out," John McClure lists four types of
"narrative preaching."[3] McClure's categories are, of course, broad,
but they are helpful in suggesting models one might appropriate if
wishing to preach narratively.

The first type of narrative preaching occurs when the "narrative
aspects of the Biblical text are related in some way [to the sermon]."
In other words, narrative preaching includes sermons in which the
form of the sermon is intentionally shaped by the form of a narrative

text. A second type, suggests McClure, comes from sermons that follow the structure of a short story or movie. Edmund Steimle observes that, "Every sermon should have something of the dramatic form of a play or short story: tightly knit, one part leading into and dependent upon the next, with some possibility of suspense and surprise in the development."[4] In recent years, Eugene Lowry has developed Steimle's proposal into the "homiletical plot."

A third classification for narrative preaching, notes McClure, is when "preachers are told to use their imagination and learn to think metaphorically in order to name grace in human experience." In this model the sermon is shaped not only by the genre of story, but by the preacher's *imagination.* Fred Craddock, for example, maintains that inductive preaching and the work of the imagination are more effective in communicating the gospel than a deductive model based on argument. McClure's final category stresses the potential for narrative to shape a church's theological worldview—in other words, sermons that refer to "faith-stories that are generated in a congregational context." Edmund Steimle, in the book *Preaching the Story,* writes of such a style where a sermon is defined by the intersection between the world of the preacher, the congregation, and the biblical text.

While most people have applauded the work of Craddock, Steimle, and Lowry, others in recent years have questioned its theological implications. Charles Campbell, for example, has argued that narrative preaching, while full of good intentions, overemphasizes the human "story" at the cost of the "story" of Jesus Christ. "The problem," writes Campbell, "is that up until now narrative homiletics has provided no resources for thinking carefully about the ways preaching contributes to the upbuilding of the church . . . *beyond* the individual hearer."[5]

In this chapter, Thomas Long offers questions that assist in unpacking the particular literary characteristics of a narrative text; Eugene Lowry describes "the homiletical plot," as well as specific designs for narrative sermons; Fred Craddock clarifies what makes a sermon "inductive"; Edmund Steimle suggests intersections a narrative preacher might observe; and Charles Campbell points to where a narrative sermon might go astray.

Thomas G. Long: Preaching a Narrative Text

Sunday morning scripture selections usually head straight for the narratives: Joseph and his brothers, Jacob wrestling with the angel, Jesus and the wedding at Cana. Narratives offer the preacher raw material from which to craft a sermon: characters, conflict, and actions and words that can be interpreted. But to preach a narrative text *faithfully*, Thomas G. Long suggests we need to attend to the specific literary characteristics of a narrative text. To discern these characteristics, we ask of the text two questions: 1) What is the rhetorical function of this narrative? 2) What literary devices does this genre employ to achieve its rhetorical effect?[6]

1) *What is the rhetorical function of this narrative?* Long believes a story impacts a listener in one of two ways. First, it encourages the listener to identify with one of the characters in the story. For example, we read how Mary and Martha entertained Jesus and imagine ourselves in the room and how we might respond.[7] Fred Craddock adds, "Those who write plays know that the key to holding interest and making an impact . . . lies in the identification of the audience with characters and critical events portrayed."[8] Choosing what character to spotlight is a first step in preaching a narrative text.

Second, a story impacts the reader by making claims on how we live our lives. For example, after reading about Joseph and his brothers are we suddenly drawn to call a sibling we haven't spoken to in months? Long writes, "Each new story is placed alongside the old stories for comparison. Sometimes the new story confirms our worldview, but on other occasions it challenges that world—and we must choose in which world we will live."[9]

2) *What literary devices does this genre employ to achieve its rhetorical effect?* In any text that employs narrative, certain "dynamics" or "devices" must be considered. Long suggests we pay particular attention to these:

> *Narrative techniques:* Notice who is telling the story. "In general," writes Long, "biblical narrators are both in the background and omniscient. . . . [Therefore] the question becomes, When is the reader informed?"[10] For example, in the very first line of the Gospel of Mark the narrator reveals Jesus is the son of God. How does the placement of this information shape the rest of the gospel?[11]
>
> *Character development:* What changes do the characters experience? What roles do they play in the story? For example, does the character have depth or is he a stereotype? Is he a complex individual like Paul or does he perform a specific role like King Herod?[12]

Plot Designs: Each story usually has a plot comprised of a beginning, a middle, and an end. How do these three parts interact? What is emphasized and what is left out?[13]

Word Choice: Are certain words unique or unusual? Do they carry particular meaning within the entire canon of scripture?[14]

Location: Where is the narrative taking place? It this important to the story?[15]

Parallel Stories: Long writes, "Biblical stories are sometimes designed to remind us of other narratives."[16] To what other narratives does this text point?

Placement of the Story: What role does this specific passage have in relationship to the narrative flow of the entire book?

Long's approach invites a preacher to engage a narrative text with the thoroughness of a literary critic and the imagination of a poet. His questions remind us that in order to preach a narrative faithfully we must grapple with its "devices" and "dynamics." We will devote an entire chapter to this style later in the book.

Eugene Lowry: The Homiletical Plot

In Eugene Lowry's *The Homiletical Plot*, he writes, "Can you imagine a playwright telling in advance how the story will end? . . . The term *plot* is key both to sermon preparation and to sermon presentation."[17] "Central, then, to what defines a narrative sermon," writes Lowry, "is *sequence.*"[18] While Long offers questions we might ask of a narrative text, Lowry's approach is primarily for nonnarrative texts. He writes, "I do not utilize the five-step process when preaching a biblical narrative sermon. The reason is clear: the biblical narrative already has its own plot."[19] Lowry's model includes five steps:

1) *Oops!: Upsetting the equilibrium:* The first task of a preacher is to present a problem, an idea, that raises questions or conflict. Lowry calls this the "itch," "the human predicament," that seeks to hold a congregation's attention.

2) *Ugh!: Analyzing the discrepancy:* Lowry believes "the greatest weakness of the average sermon is the weakness of diagnosis."[20] This part of the sermon elaborates on the issues and tensions raised in the beginning of the sermon and how they relate to our lives.

3) *Aha!: Disclosing the clue to resolution:* At this point, the preacher offers a solution based in the gospel that ideally comes as a surprise or "reversal."

4) *Whee!: Experiencing the gospel:* The good news arises as a counterpoint to the problems raised in steps one and two. Lowry writes, "Seldom in preparing a sermon have I had difficulty in discerning what the gospel had to say about the issue at hand . . . the problem [was usually] that I had not probed deeply enough in my diagnosis."[21]

5) *Yeah!: Anticipating the consequences:* The final step is addressing what happens after the benediction. Lowry writes, "The critical matter left for explication has to do with the future—now made new by the gospel."[22]

Ronald Allen remarks that the strength of Lowry's method is that it "encourages a church to name and analyze a disequilibrium that has taken place in the community."[23] Lowry's model does not shy away from problem areas that can arise in a congregation or a text. Rather, the model affirms these questions and understands that to leave them unaddressed would be counter to the character of the gospel.

Eugene Lowry: Four Designs for Narrative Sermons

In *How to Preach a Parable*, Lowry moves from a theoretical to practical model of narrative preaching and offers four templates to place over a text. Lowry writes, "Choosing from the several options of sermonic design is not the first step in the formation of a narrative sermon—it is the central task."[24] Lowry's four options include:

1) *Running the Story:* In this model both the text and the shape of the sermon are interwoven. "The preacher will highlight," writes Lowry, "elaborate, amplify, and creatively enflesh certain portions while moving through the text."[25]

2) *Delaying the story:* In certain sermons, a preacher might delay the story, in particular if it offers a resolution to issues or conflicts raised in the sermon. "Sometimes," writes Lowry, "there are pastoral reasons to begin a sermon with a current congregational concern, then turn to the text for resolution."[26]

3) *Suspending the story:* Sometimes a helpful approach is to begin with the text but then step out of the narrative flow to address a particular concern. Lowry explains that, "It may be that the preacher will move to a contemporary situation in order to 'find a way out' of issues the text raises.[27] The preacher then returns to the text and concludes the sermon."

4) *Alternating the story:* The final approach divides the narrative portion of the text into "sections, episodes, or vignettes, with other kinds of material filling in around the biblical story."[28]

The model we choose is determined by the focus of the text and whether this issue is best explored and resolved "in the text, or before it, or after it, or outside it." "Once the sermonic intention is clear," writes Lowry, the hard work is done and "other kinds of preparation steps fall into place."[29]

Fred Craddock: The Inductive Sermon

In 1971, Craddock took stock of the current approaches towards preaching and set off in a new direction. At the time most preaching was "deductive," focusing on a proposition later developed into three points. Craddock observed, however, that people don't live deductively. He commented that, "Everyone lives inductively. . . . No farmer deals with the problem of calfdom, only with the calf."[30] Craddock saw there might be room for a style of preaching that involved the listeners' imagination. He called this style "inductive." "Simply stated," writes Craddock, "deductive movement is from the general truth to the particular application or experience while inductive is the reverse."[31] In an inductive sermon, "thought moves from the particulars of experience that have a familiar ring in the listener's ear to a general truth or conclusion."[32] In other words, the congregation is invited to "retrace" the journey the pastor has taken in crafting the sermon with the intention to "see if [the congregation] comes to that same conclusion."[33]

Three skills are required to become an "inductive" preacher. 1) Cultivate the ability to notice and re-create "concrete experiences." 2) Structure the sermon like a "good story or a good joke" and build anticipation. Craddock remarks that, "The period between the father's announcement of a family trip and the trip itself may be the children's greatest happiness."[34] 3) Allow the listener to complete the sermon. The preacher does not "throw the ball and catch it himself." As a model, Craddock points to Jesus and the fact that "Jesus' preaching depended not simply on the revelatory power of his parables but also upon the perceptive power of those who attended to them."[35]

Fred Craddock gazed into the homiletical forest and found a new path in the midst of well-worn trails. He understood the preparation for preaching involved not only exegetical work but a sensitivity to how a sermon would be received. He asked questions like, "How do we listen?" "What is the best way to communicate the gospel?" The answers compelled him to open the door of his study, and invite the congregation to have a seat.

Edmund Steimle: The Fabric of the Sermon

Thomas Long notes that Edmund Steimle "was in the middle of, and to some degree was the cause of, a major shift in American preaching."[36] Steimle observed that good preaching paid attention to the intersection of three stories: the stories of the text, the preacher, and the congregation. The preacher's challenge was to "interpret the biblical story [so] that light is shed on all three stories."[37]

In his essay, "The Fabric of the Sermon," Steimle offers five steps a preacher might take to weave a narrative sermon. 1) Pay attention to and highlight the secular, "so that what is heard on Sunday morning will also make some sense on Sunday afternoon, to say nothing of Monday morning."[38] 2) Ask questions the congregation is already asking. 3) Craft a sermon that takes the form of a "story told, as a whole and in its parts."[39] 4) Be inductive. Steimle agreed with Craddock that a sermon should be "low-keyed, which leaves the issue in the air rather than pushing a person into a corner."[40] 5) And be "lean and spare" with your language. "From the great stories of the Old Testament, Abraham, Jacob, Jonah, to the parables of Jesus . . . the fabric is that of stories told crisply, sometimes rough-hewn, always quickly and surely to the point."[41]

For Steimle a narrative sermon is grounded in stories that shape a congregation: stories from the Bible, from church members, from the preacher. A preacher is above all a good conversation partner, listening for stories both fit and appropriate.

Charles Campbell: Jesus as Story

While recognizing the contribution of narrative preaching, Campbell argues such preaching is nonetheless theologically questionable when it guides a congregation towards the human condition instead of God. He points to Craddock, Steimle, and Lowry and discerns a troubling emphasis on human experience. He writes,

One reads the literature with the impression that, where the sermon is concerned, the church is simply a rather loose collection of individuals who share similar experiences and participate in the event of oral communication. Although everyone affirms at least in passing the importance of stories in forming communal identity, the focus remains on individual experience. No consideration is given to the Christian faith as a set of communal practices and skills, including linguistic ones, and to the ways in which preaching functions at this level.[42]

In his helpful article on Campbell's work, David Lose observes that for Campbell the goal of preaching is to proclaim "the story of Jesus, not the particulars of human experience."[43] Campbell's intent is "to reverse the direction or flow of the sermon away from human experience, and towards the biblical reality rendered by the narrative."[44]

While the deans of narrative preaching would probably disagree about their intention being to emphasize the human experience, Campbell does helpfully remind us that narrative preaching must always be grounded in the text and in the story of Jesus Christ. Richard Lischer is right when he cautions that, "the church is not saved by stories but by the God who is rendered by them and emerges by their means."[45]

SERMONS

"The Lamb King"

Peter Hoytema   Revelation 5:1–14

No man is an island. No one except for John, that is. Look at him. He is elderly now, his beard gray and flowing. He stands, slightly stooped, the waves of many years having crashed against him. It is dusk when he looks heavenward, craning his neck to see what might yet be true for an old man suspended somewhere between the earth of his solitude and the sky of rapturous worship. Alone, he gazes at vision after vision splayed like sunsets across the sky.

And he weeps. Make no mistake, John's face is wet from more than the misty evening air. Mingled with the salt of sea spray is the salt of his tears. They flow, as irrepressible as the waves that break on the shore of Patmos. Down through the furrows chiseled by the years into his cheeks they fall, eventually splashing on the ground below. The breaking point has come.

Is this any way for the beloved disciple to retire, spending the sunset of his life banished, as if to some hard-as-rock place we dare to call a "rest home," years of service behind him with only a vision of possibilities ahead? Seeing John as he is, his chest heaving, his head bobbing, his sandaled feet stamping, one is tempted to conclude that the disciple Jesus loved has become the disciple Jesus lost. He appears to be as deserted as Patmos itself.

And it's all because of that vision, that wonderful, terrible vision. No sooner does one vision end and this one begins. No sooner does the sky shrink, stifling the echoes of the chorus, "You are worthy, our Lord and God, to receive glory and honor and power . . . ," and suddenly no one is found worthy. Not in heaven, not on earth, not under the earth. The sky, having been churned by the thunder of the mighty angel's question, "Who is worthy to open the scroll and break its seals?" is suddenly, ominously calm. The ensuing silence is as deafening as the question itself.

Is this God's idea of a cruel joke, whereby God apparently sets John up by floating him to the heights of God's potential only to plunge him down to the depths of creaturely inability? Why must the hope of God's triumph always seem to dissolve in the tears of human brokenness? Why must the soil of our faith be persistently eroded by the surge of sorrow, of disappointment, of loss? Why?

We have all asked these questions because we have all stood where

John stood. Like him, we know what it is to stand suspended between a rock and a hard place. We feel his grief whenever we perceive brokenness around or within us and are confronted by the reality of our inability to mend what is broken. We all know well enough that life is not always what it is supposed to be, that none of us is completely insulated from the pain of life in a fallen world. Even more than this, we recognize within ourselves a natural tendency to try and fix whatever we perceive to be broken, or if we can't, to try and find someone or something that will.

A career health-care professional, suddenly victimized by corporate downsizing and faced with the prospect of unemployment at age forty-six, has stood where John has stood. A woman, rocked by her husband's confession of infidelity, whose pleas for reconciliation do nothing to curb his waywardness, has stood where John has stood. The angular, bespectacled third-grader who day after day sustains the mockery of playground bullies has stood where John has stood.

Who is able to rid our lives of things such as these? Who is worthy to take the script of our lives, break its seals, and pronounce healing where there is soreness, peace where there is division, mercy where there is sin? We know we cannot do these things. We are too small. Reminders of our smallness lap against our shores constantly. But is there no one worthy enough to do these things, no one in heaven, on earth, or under the earth? Beyond our troubles themselves, is not our deepest trouble the fear that nothing can be done about them?

Consider the physically disabled, for instance. Undoubtedly, few among us are confronted by this trouble as frequently as they. Like islands in the sea of our frenzied, close-of-the-century lifestyle, they stand out among us as those who, like John on Patmos, are banished, apparently forgotten. Take a few moments sometime to observe their plight. Notice how ill-prepared our world is to accommodating them, how they must struggle to make their way through our doors, up our stairs, across our streets, and over our curbs.

Not long ago I watched an elderly woman in a motorized wheelchair making her way down a busy sidewalk. Her bony hand controlled the accelerator as persistently she had to adjust her speed to avoid running into pedestrians seemingly oblivious to her presence. I adjusted the pace of my walk too as I deliberately sought to maintain a constant distance behind her, watching, absorbing as much of her difficulty as I could. Lines in the sidewalk jolted her. She had to alter the course of her travel to find ramps that would gain her access to places she would otherwise reach by a much shorter, more direct means of entry. The "whirring" sound of her motorized wheelchair reminded me of the sound of my blender, but the irony here was that there was to be blending for her at all. The disabled, apparently, are too small to notice, too broken to care for. Beyond their obvious troubles, I wonder whether their deepest trouble is the fear that nothing can be done about them. The face of the elderly woman in the wheelchair persuaded me to think that, at least for her, this was so.

Who is worthy to break the seals of this script and change it back to the way it ought to be? Who is able to pronounce judgment where judgment is warranted, and healing where healing is needed? This is the angel's question, and it is our question too. It rumbles through our lives as surely as it shook the sky above Patmos, reducing us at times to the image of John who waits and weeps, who falls apart just as surely as the scroll he sees remains sealed.

It's not until we hear another voice, that belonging to one of the elders in the vision, that a wonderful transition begins to take place. God sustains broken people with a vision of God's victory. At first one wouldn't know it. John is told to dry his tears. The elder's announcement, "See, the Lion of the tribe of Judah, the root of David, has conquered, so that he can open the scroll and its seven seals," proclaims the victory of God. John straightens his back and arches his eyebrows as again he cranes his neck upwards, expectantly waiting for the introduction of God's conquering hero.

And what does he see but a lamb, standing as if it had been slaughtered. This is the victorious one, a docile lamb that bears the mark of slaughter on its neck, its white wool stained and matted with its own dried blood? Where is the lion we are told about, the strong and stately creature we expect to see, its head held high, its mane blowing elegantly in the wind? At first this appears to be nothing like a vision of God's victory, this lamb that apparently does nothing more than bleat its way to martyrdom.

But upon further investigation, we begin to discover much more than this. If we are willing to stand beside John as more of this vision unfolds, we will see that this slaughtered Lamb, this apparent image of weakness, is itself the image of God's victory. It is from the wool of this Lamb that God knits our salvation. God sustains broken people with vision of God's own brokenness through which this victory is accomplished.

There is nothing about a slaughtered lamb that evokes the kind of worship we see in this vision, except this: the fact that by the blood of this Lamb saints from every tribe and language and people and nation are ransomed for God; the fact that this Lamb is worthy to take the scroll and open its seals precisely because it was slaughtered, its blood its credentials. God sustains broken people with a vision of God's victory. The martyred Lamb is resurrected as the Lion of the tribe of Judah.

This brokenness of God speaks to our brokenness, the victory of God that speaks to our healing, the impending triumph that God has yet to extend into our lives. It is not the way of the world. Our world has no place for lambs but the slaughterhouse. Their meekness will persistently be rejected as people opt for the impressiveness of the lion. What Disney executive would ever have suggested making a movie titled *The Lamb King?* Yet this is God's way. God sustains broken people with a vision of God's victory. A triumphant victory, a quiet victory. A convincing victory won in and through apparent weakness.

Every once in a while we too catch a glimpse of this vision. God's ways persistently break against our world like the waves on the shore, and every once in a while we notice what is happening. During a flight I read an article written by W. P. Kinsella, the Canadian writer whose novel, *Shoeless Joe*, was the inspiration behind the acclaimed movie *Field of Dreams*. Do you remember it? It was the surreal film that told the story of a farmer who hears and ultimately obeys the disembodied voice that instructs him to build a baseball diamond on his property.

It seems the baseball field the directors carved out of the cornfields just outside Dyersville, Iowa, is still there. Now, more than a decade later, it remains, an island among the waves of corn in the American heartland. In fact, it has become somewhat of a shrine. Each year thousands of people make their pilgrimage to Dyersville, hoping to forget themselves for a little while and play in this field of dreams. In the article, Kinsella describes what transpired when he last visited the baseball diamond. He watched from the bleachers as four young men played on the field. Unlike the usual visitors, who arrived dressed in uniforms and cleats, these four were bikers, dressed in leather jackets. They hollered to each other as they ran around the bases and fired the ball around the diamond. It was dusk, the time of day movie directors often refer to as "magic time" since the dying of the light produces an array of pale hues in the evening sky.

As the sun was setting, a car pulled into the parking lot and a father and son walked slowly to the field. The boy looked to be about ten years old and walked with crutches. As the father walked past Kinsella he smiled and said, "He's just got to have a quick look at the field. We've come all the way from Kansas City and we'll be back first thing in the morning."

They stood by the side of the field when finally one of the bikers asked if the boy wanted to play. The father helped his son to the batter's box and one of the bikers pitched while the others covered the bases. With his father supporting him from behind, the boy managed to hit a ball back to the pitcher. Everyone on the diamond cheered in praise of the boy's accomplishment. The pitcher then approached the father and the two men talked for a moment. The biker signaled to a friend who came and held the boy while the father stood to the side. Once again the boy hit a slow bouncer to the infield, but this time his father reacted by scooping him up and running with him to first base. Kinsella writes, "the second baseman managed to misplay the ball enough that the father was able to plant his son on first base before the ball got there. There were high fives all around as the sun disappeared."[46]

What W. P. Kinsella saw that night is the very same thing John saw in the vision that appeared in the "magic time" of dusk on Patmos. It is what we see whenever God sustains us with a vision of God's victory that breaks through the reality of our smallness, elevating us from our banishment and isolation to a place of community, of grace, and of God's tranquil power. In this place it is true, no one is an island. For by the blood of the Lamb saints from every tribe and language and people and nation have been ransomed, and they have been made to be a kingdom and priests serving our God.

Worthy is the Lamb that was slaughtered to receive power and wealth and wisdom and might and honor and glory and blessing. Amen.

Peter Hoytema is the senior pastor at Midland Park Christian Reformed Church in Midland Park, New Jersey. This sermon was preached on July 24, 1998, at the Montgomery Memorial Chapel, San Francisco Theological Seminary.

"When the Roll Is Called Down Here"

Fred Craddock   Romans 16

I hope you will not feel guilty if your heart was not all a-flutter during the reading of the text. It's not very interesting. It's a list of names, a list of strange names. I always tell my students in preaching class, "When you're preaching from biblical texts, avoid the lists. They're deadly. Don't preach from the lists." It seems that Paul is calling the roll. That's a strange thing in itself. I have never worshiped in a church in which anyone got up and called the roll. It could be very dull. Well, it could. . . . It could be interesting in a way.

Calling the roll sometimes is not all that bad. Last December I was summoned to Superior Court, DeKalb County, Georgia, to serve on the jury. On Monday morning at nine o'clock, 240 of us would be chosen. The deputy clerk of the Superior Court stood and called the roll. Two hundred and forty names. She did not have them in alphabetical order. You had to listen. And while I was listening, I began to *listen*. There were two Bill Johnsons. One was black and one was white, and they were both Bill Johnson. There was a man named Clark, a Mr. Clark, who answered when the clerk read "Mrs. Clark." He said, "Here." And she looked up and said, "Mrs. Clark." And he said, "Here." And she said, "*Mrs.* Clark." And he stood up and said, "Well, I thought the letter was for me, and I opened it." And she said, "We summoned Mrs. Clark." And he said, "Well, I'm here. Can't I do it? She doesn't have any interest in this sort of thing." And the clerk said, "Mr. Clark, how do you know? She doesn't even know she's been summoned."

This roll call *was* pretty good. There was a man there whose name I wrote down phonetically because I couldn't spell it. His name was Zerfel Lashenstein. I remember it because they went over it five or six times, mispronouncing it. He insisted it be pronounced correctly and finally stood in a huff and said, "I see no reason why I should serve on a jury in a court that can't pronounce my name." The woman next to me said, "Lie-shen-stein. I wonder if he's a Jew?" I said, "Well, I don't know. Could be. Does it matter?" And she said, "I am German. My name is Zeller." And I said, "Well, it doesn't matter. That was forty years ago." And she said, "He and I could be seated next to each other in a jury." I said, "Well, you were probably just a child when all that happened years ago." And she said, "I was ten years old. I visited Grandmother. She lived about four miles from Buchenwald. I smelled the odor."

You know, a person could get interested in Paul's calling the roll. Even if it's no more than to say, "I wonder how Paul knew all those people since he had never been to the church?" I wonder if back then you could buy mailing lists? After all, he wants to raise money in Rome for his Spanish mission, and he is politically wise.

He says, "Tell this one hello and that one hello." Some scholars think this doesn't even belong in Romans. He's never been to Rome. But I'm interested in the roll call because it gives a kind of sociological profile of the membership of the church.

Now, I don't expect you to remember, but in the list there is a husband and wife, Aquila and Priscilla. There's a man and his mother, Rufus and his mother. There is a brother and sister, Nereus and his sisters, Tryphaena and Tryphosa. There is an old man, Epaenetus. Isn't that an interesting profile of the church? There is a single woman, Mary. There's a single man, Herodian. Not a lot of nuclear family there at all, except as Christ has called them together. It's an interesting list, sort of. Not very.

But for Paul it's not a list. Don't call it a list. He's packing his stuff. He's in the home of Gaius in Corinth, who is host to Paul and host to the church in Corinth. Paul is getting ready to go west to Italy and Spain. He's about to move to a new parish, one far away. He is now about fifty-nine years old, I would guess. He feels he has one more good ministry in him. Most churches don't want a person fifty-nine years old, but those churches had no choice, because Paul started his own. He wants to have one other ministry because he got a late start. He was probably about thirty-five when he started. He doesn't have much to pack: his coat and his books and a few things. And while he is throwing things away to trim down the load for packing and moving, he comes across some notes and some correspondence, and he sits down among the boxes and begins to remember. Don't call it a list.

You've done it yourself. When my wife and I finished our service at the student church when in seminary, our last Sunday there they gave us a gift. It was a quilt some of the women of the church had made, and they stitched into the top of the quilt the names of all the church members. And every time we move and we come across that quilt, we spread it out on the bed and we start remembering. We remember something about everyone: there's Chester, who voted against and persuaded others to vote against my raise. There's Mary and John, who put new tires on our car. There's Loy, very quiet, never said anything. There is his wife, Marie. There is this marvelous woman, Loyce, lived with that man who drank and became violent, and yet she was always faithful and pleasant. And he was dying of cancer when we went—my first funeral there, you remember. This is the way we go over the quilt. Don't call it a list.

Paul said, "Don't call it a list. Aquila and Priscilla, they risked their necks for me. Andronicus and Junias, we were in jail together. Phew!

They're great Christians. There's Mary. Mary worked hard. She was there when everybody else quit. She's the one who always said, 'Now, Paul, you go on home; I'll put things up. I'll put the hymnals away, and I'll pick up all the papers and straighten the chairs. You go on home; you're tired.' 'Well, Mary, you're tired too.' 'Yes, Paul, but you've got to ride a donkey across Asia tomorrow. You go on. I'll pick up here.' Mary worked hard.

"Epaenetus, the first person converted under my preaching, and I didn't sleep a wink that night saying, 'Thank God. Finally somebody heard.' The first one to respond to the gospel. What a marvelous day that was! Tryphaena and Tryphosa, obviously twins. You hear it, don't you, in the names? Tryphaena and Tryphosa. They always sat on this side, and they both wore blue every Sunday. I never knew them apart, really. One of them had a mole on her cheek, but I didn't know if it was Tryphaena or Tryphosa. I never did get them straight. And Rufus. Tell Rufus hello, and tell his mother hello, because she's my mother, too."

Isn't that something? Some woman earned from this apostle the title "Mother." Can't you see her, this woman able to be mother to Paul? Probably stayed in their home. She was a rather large woman. Always had an apron, a lot of things stuffed in the pocket of the apron, hair pulled back in a bun. Fixed a good breakfast. Paul said, "I'm sorry. I can't stay. I have to be on my way." "Sit down and eat your breakfast. I don't care if you are an apostle, you've got to eat." "Tell my mother hello." This is not a list.

I remember when they brought the famous list to Atlanta. The workers set it up in the public place, block after block to form a long wall of names. Vietnam names. Some of us looked at it as if it were a list of names. Others went over closer. Some walked slowly down the column. There was a woman who went up and put her finger on a name, and she held a child up and put the child's hand on a name. There was a woman who kissed the wall at a name. There were flowers lying beneath the wall. Don't call it a list. It's not a list.

In fact these names in Romans 16 are for Paul extremely special, because even though he says, "Say hello to," what he is really saying is good-bye. Oh, he's going to Rome, he says. But before he goes to Rome, he has to go to Jerusalem. He's going with the offering, and he's going into a nest of hostility. And so at the end of chapter 15, he says to these people, "Pray with me. Agonize with me, that I won't be killed in Jerusalem, that the saints will accept the money in Jerusalem, that I'll get to come back and be with you. Please pray." These are not just names.

Do you have a piece of paper? Well, use your worship bulletin. Would you write in the margin somewhere or at the bottom these words: "I thank my God for all my remembrance of you." And write a name.

You choose the name. You remember the name. Write another name, and another name, and another name.

Before I married and was serving a little mission in the Appalachians, I moved in my service down to a place on Watts Bar Lake, between Chattanooga and Knoxville—a little village. It was the custom in that church at Easter to have a baptismal service. My church immerses, and this baptismal service was held in Watts Bar Lake on Easter evening at sundown. Out on a sandbar, I, with the candidates for baptism, moved into the water, and then they moved across to the shore, where the little congregation was gathered singing around the fire and cooking supper. They had constructed little booths for changing clothes, with blankets hanging, and as the candidates moved from the water, they went in and changed clothes and went to the fire in the center. And finally, last of all I went over and changed clothes and went to the fire.

Once we were all around the fire, this is the ritual of that tradition: Glenn Hickey, always, Glenn introduced the new people, gave their names, where they lived, and their work. Then the rest of us formed a circle around them while they stayed warm at the fire. The ritual was each person in the circle gave her or his name and said this: "My name is _____, and if you ever need somebody to do washing and ironing." "My name is _____, and if you ever need somebody to chop wood." "My name is _____ if you ever need anybody to babysit." "My name is _____ if you ever need anybody to repair your house for you." "My name is _____ if you ever need anybody to sit with the sick." "My name is _____ if you ever need a car to go to town." And around the circle. Then we ate, and then we had a square dance. And at a time they knew—I didn't know—Percy Miller, with thumbs in his bibbed overalls, would stand up and say, "It's time to go." Everybody left, and he lingered behind and with his big shoe kicked sand over the dying fire.

At my first experience of that, he saw me standing there still. He looked at me and said, "Craddock, folks don't ever get any closer than this." In that little community, they have a name for that. I've heard it in other communities, too. In that community, their name for that is *church*. They call that church.

Have you written any names? Do you have a name or two? Keep the list. *Keep* the list, because to you it's not a list. In fact, the next time you move, keep that. Even if you have to leave your car and your library and your furniture and your typewriter and everything else, take that with you. In fact, when your ministry is ended and you leave the earth, take it with you.

I know, I know, I know. When you get to the gate St. Peter's going to say, "Now, look, you went into the world with nothing, you gotta come out of it with nothing. Now what have you got?" And you say, "Well, it's just some names." "Well, let me see it." "Well, now this is just some names of folk I worked with and folk who helped me." "Well, let me see it." "Well, this is just a group of people that if it weren't for them, I'd have never made it." He says, "I want to see it." And he smiles and says, "I know all of them. In fact, on my way here to the gate I passed a group. They were painting a big, red sign to hang over the street, and it said, 'Welcome Home'."

Fred Craddock is the author of As One Without Authority, Overhearing the Gospel, *and* Preaching. *He has also written several other commentaries and resources for interpreting the Bible.*

Chapter 2

African American Preaching

The sermon is different from other staged events because it seeks to tilt life Godward, to encourage us to answer as we are addressed by God.

Samuel Proctor[1]

Introduction

*I*n *The Color of Water,* James McBride describes his childhood pastor's sermons as starting "like a tiny choo-choo train and ending up like a roaring locomotive."[2] From Martin Luther King Jr. on the Capitol steps to small congregations like James McBride's, African American preachers have crafted a unique preaching style of celebration and rhetorical flair.

"Today," writes James Harris, "there are black preachers who retain vestiges of the past . . . whose voice thunders like the roar of mighty wind."[3] Men and women such as Henry and Ella Pearson Mitchell, Gardner Taylor, and Samuel Proctor have modeled in the pulpit and in the seminary classroom strategies that are in many ways unique to African Americans. In this chapter, Henry Mitchell reminds us to preach *good news* and sift for the details of a text; Samuel Proctor suggests a "dialectic" approach; Martin Luther King Jr. demonstrates the value of appropriating our homiletical tradition; James Harris offers a homiletic of liberation; and Evans Crawford describes a model of preaching as partnership.

Henry Mitchell: The Celebration of Preaching

A seminary president recently admitted after traveling through the country he longed for a sermon that left a congregation with a bounce in their step. Too often we try to be clever, he said, when all people long to hear is God loves and forgives them. In *Celebration and Experience in Preaching*, Henry Mitchell suggests the greatest mistake a preacher can make is forgetting that above all the message of the Bible is *good news*.

To craft a celebratory sermon, Mitchell recommends saving our finest thought, our "best verbal poetry," for our final moments in the pulpit.[4] In the African American tradition, the peak of the celebration is always left for the conclusion. Mitchell writes,

> No matter how misused by some or criticized by others, the celebration at its best is the goal to which all of the Black sermon is moving. In sermon preparation, it is often the celebration that is chosen right after a text and purpose have been selected. It is on the basis of the final celebration more than any other element that the sermon will be judged. If the sermon is remembered, then it will be because the text was etched by ecstasy on the heart of the hearer.[5]

While some traditions emphasize ending a sermon with a challenge to mission or discipleship, Mitchell advises we strike the "we ought's" from the "climax" and conclude with a word of comfort, a word of grace, a word that leaves one praising God.[6]

While most in the African American tradition resonate with Mitchell's emphasis, others do express caution. James Harris, for example, writes that, "Black preaching is indeed exciting and jubilant, but it is also sad and reflective. It represents the ebb and flow of the Holy Spirit that correlates with the ups and down of life. . . . It is creative interplay between joy and sorrow, freedom and oppression, justice and injustice."[7] In Mitchell's defense, he does not guide the preacher away from sorrow and injustice, but rather advocates that our final words be wrapped in grace and not judgment. A sermon addresses the spectrum of what it means to be human, but above all we are in the business of *good news*.

The Art of Details

Another characteristic of African American preaching is its detailed portrayal of a biblical text or character. The effectiveness of this sketch, Mitchell notes, depends on whether or not one has read "about David or Paul so long and with such interest that eventually it is as if one grew up on the same block with him. It takes scholarship, in most cases, to dig up the tiny details that enable Biblical characters to come to life."[8] Barbara

Brown Taylor adds, "If God is in the details, then every detail of this life is worth listening to." Details, both in the biblical text and in our choice of nouns, verbs, and adjectives, are the lifeblood of preaching. Mitchell writes,

> There is a great need for more vivid but not less valid details, often not given in the Bible or anywhere else. These details help the hearer to be caught up in the experience being narrated and, as a result, to understand better and to be moved to change. Black preaching, at its best, is rich in the imaginative supply of these details and in their dramatic use in telling the Gospel stories.[9]

In order to capture the essence of Jesus' birth, writes Mitchell, "the hay in the manger is crucial."[10]

Samuel Proctor: A Dialectical Approach

While Henry Mitchell has encouraged celebration and the importance of details in the text, Samuel Proctor spent his life prodding preachers to cultivate an instinct for sermon design. He believed the crafting of a sermon should always follow "an orderly, productive, tested procedure."[11] The procedure is developed by approaching a sermon's structure with the curiosity of a physician. "A serious preacher," writes Proctor, "will be concerned about the anatomy of each sermon . . . because the sermon's structure will determine largely how well the message it bears will be conveyed."[12] The structure Proctor advocated was suggested by the categories of G.W.F. Hegel's dialectical approach. This model includes the following steps:

> Introduction (Antithesis) } The claim
> Transition (Thesis)
> Relevant Question – So What
> Synthesis – What Now

Proctor taught his students to begin their sermon preparation by focusing on a *proposition*, a sentence that succinctly states the sermon's purpose. This proposition is a "faith statement, not a newscast or a book review. . . . It is a positive, affirmative statement. It is good news, the proclamation of what God can bring out of any situation or event."[13] A proposition might be, "God is present in human affairs and seeks to bring something redemptive out of every situation." Or, "Justice, fairness, and compassion are prerequisites for community, and Christian community in Jesus' name challenges all forms of injustice."[14]

With a proposition in hand, Proctor asks the preacher to imagine why this sermon needs to be preached. The answer is called the "*antithesis*." He writes, "There was always a reason for preaching a certain theme . . . a mood of despair that had to be dissipated, a sin that called for repentance, a dullness of spirit that needed the water of life, or a hunger for righteousness waiting for living bread."[15] In Proctor's model, one begins the sermon with the "antithesis . . . because it usually has the best chance to capture the listener's attention."[16] After the issues of the antithesis have been raised, we then introduce the "thesis," or solution. Proctor believed a strong thesis was crucial; without it a congregation's attention would wander.

With an antithesis and thesis in place, the next step is to ask, "So what?" This is what Proctor calls *the relevant question*, a question that anticipates the congregation's doubts and concerns. For example, if preaching on the text where Jesus claims no one will die before he returns, it would be foolish to preach on anything other than that the disciples did die before Jesus' return. Proctor writes, "[the relevant question] attempts to lock the sermon on course, to avoid drift and sway, to keep it *one* sermon and not many."[17]

Once the course of the sermon has been set, "the body of the sermon," writes Proctor, "is—the synthesis—[and] is made up of *answers to the relevant question*."[18] As an example, Proctor offers a sermon structure for the parable of the sower in Mark 4:3–8. The *proposition*, writes Proctor, might be that "we should offer the gospel to everyone because we can never tell where it will take root and multiply." The *antithesis* would be: "No matter how we go about it, some persons reject the Good News." In response, the *thesis* is, "If we keeping sowing, some seeds will fall on the ground and multiply." And the *relevant question*: "What strategies does this parable suggest for us who share the gospel in our society today?" The *synthesis* then takes each example of sowing seeds and examines what it reveals about sharing the gospel.[19]

Martin Luther King Jr.: Unity of Tradition

Henry Mitchell remarks that, "One of the most intriguing questions about Black preaching is, how did the early preachers manage to learn how to preach at all, let alone so well?[20] The answer he believes is African Americans have always "served a kind of apprenticeship, sometimes formal but more often informal, under a known master of the craft of preaching."[21]

In his book *The Preacher King,* Richard Lischer relates that Martin Luther King Jr. continually drew upon the tradition that preceded and surrounded him. Lischer writes that King collected, "for his day-to-day preaching and speech making . . . a canon of titles, basic outlines, and thematic formulas, ranging from the epigram to the extended set piece, which he moved from speech to speech and worked into *any* address as the occasion demanded."[22] Lischer discovered, for example, that King often preached a sermon entitled "The Three Dimensions of a Complete Life" that drew upon the ideas and structure of a Phillips Brooks sermon, "The Symmetry of Life." "What King borrowed," writes Lischer, "was a biblical text, a tone, and a concept for a sermon along with a generic outline consisting of three 'places,' which for obvious reasons King amplified with proofs unlike those used by Brooks."[23]

Lischer's point is not that King "stole" his homiletical material. A survey of sermons from the 1950s reveals most preachers circulated their ideas and illustrations.[24] What King teaches us, however, is a preacher who fails to become an apprentice, who ignores the craft and contribution of his predecessors and peers, ultimately denies his or her congregation the best of their homiletical tradition. "It becomes clear," writes Lischer, "that for the most part King used his peers—Fosdick, Buttrick, Thurman, Hamilton—the way preachers have always used the sermons of others: for an idea, a phrase, an outline."[25]

African American preachers are fortunate, applauds Lischer, for in their tradition they can draw upon an "enormous disassembled inventory of rhetorical parts ready for immediate installation."[26] While most of us do not possess such an "inventory," each of our particular traditions does offer a wealth of homiletical insight and style. Mitchell suggests that we "make it a point to attend services or collect tapes of good examples of the preaching event. . . . Without seeking to imitate specific preachers, allow the nuances of formation and flow in consciousness to engulf you as you listen."[27]

James Harris: A Homiletic of Liberation

The journalist Samuel Freedman spent a year with Rev. Johnny Ray Youngblood and the Saint Paul Community Baptist Church, located in one of New York City's toughest neighborhoods. He attended meetings, counseling appointments, and worship services and wrote about the life of an African American pastor. Concerning preaching he observed, "[It is] an act of syncretism and historical homage, returning to the African griot, the praise-singer, and to the slave preacher, teaching a liberation gospel after dark in the quarters."[28]

Samuel Proctor once asked, "How shall they hear?" and answered, "They will listen for a word that will release them from the fetters that have bound them."[29] African American preaching has often pointed towards injustice, demanding individual and social change. James Harris writes that "the black preacher . . . has historically been one who . . . could influence the community to mobilize its efforts towards liberation and transformation.[30] James Cone forcefully adds that, "Any starting point that ignores God in Christ as the Liberator of the oppressed or that makes salvation as liberation secondary is invalid and thus heretical."[31]

Arising from the history of slavery and discrimination, African American preaching has persistently spoken a word of hope to African Americans and to the world. Cone writes, "The biblical God . . . is the God of Jesus Christ who calls the helpless and weak into a newly created existence."[32] The preacher's charge is to proclaim a message of hope by addressing how society can be transformed. "This form of liberation preaching," writes Harris, "encourages blacks and the poor to participate in the system, to get an education, to get involved in the political process, and to do those things that will gradually help and transform society."[33]

African Americans are of course not alone in emphasizing liberation and social change. This style of preaching includes all who proclaim God desires the oppressed to be free. For example, Justo and Catherine Gonzalez write,

> The most creative theology is being done from the perspective of those who have been traditionally powerless in society . . . African Americans, Hispanics, Asian Americans, and others. . . . They experience the empowerment of the gospel, not only in an inner sense, but also in the sense that it compels and enables them to strive for justice.[34]

Those who have been powerless in society, including African Americans, remind us God will not stand for oppression. As preachers we must always work for social change by proclaiming a liberating word from the pulpit.

Evans Crawford: Preaching as Partnership

At a recent preaching conference I was startled when two African Americans shouted "Yes, Lord," or, "My, my my," as I preached. However, as this continued through the sermon, I quickly welcomed their interjections as affirmation and support. Richard Lischer notes that the "black preacher and audience . . . have at their disposal a second, nondiscursive track on which the sermon proceeds. This is the sermon's *sound track*.[35] Mitchell describes this "sound track," or the call and response in African American preaching, as a form of "creative partnership."

Evans Crawford, in his book *The Hum,* helpfully offers a list of responses he developed for students in his seminary classroom. In the class, these responses are assigned particular meanings that when spoken aloud assist a preacher in understanding whether or not the sermon is connecting with its audience. The responses include:

1) "Help 'em Lord"—means the search is on for connections, and we start out in need of prayer.
2) "Well?"—You're hinting to the witness with a chantable refrain or "riff."
3) "That's all right!"—There are Good news and gospel possibilities; the sermon is becoming persuasive.
4) "Glory, Hallelujah"—the loudest praise, highest joy, and praise to God.
5) "Amen!"—the truth is affirmed and the pitch is right for the people and Scripture passage.[36]

Crawford remarks that "all preachers, no matter what their background, would like to move their listeners from praying "Help 'em Lord!" to "Amen" and "Glory Hallelujah!"[37]

Most mainline Protestant congregations, of course, would feel uncomfortable given a crib sheet of responses to shout throughout the sermon. But might it be possible to gather a small group who would offer feedback and encouragement, before or after the service? For Crawford's list, and Mitchell's observation that preaching is "partnership," remind us we all need a pat on the back, whether from a member of such a group nodding their head as we climb into the pulpit, or even someone shouting, "Glory, Hallelujah!" or "Amen," as we sit down.

SERMONS

"She Had Neither Father nor Mother"

Valerie Brown-Troutt   Esther 2:5–7

And he brought up Hadassah, that is Esther, his uncle's daughter: for she had neither father nor mother; and the maid was fair and beautiful, whom Mordecai, when her father and mother were dead, took for his own daughter. Esther 2:7.

I want you all, especially the children and the young people, to meet Hadassah.

Excuse me while I call Hadassah so you can meet her.

Hadassah, Hadassah, Hadassah, where are you?

Hadassah, don't you hear me calling you?

Hadassah, where are you, girl?

Get in here right now, so the people can see you and meet you.

Hurry up girl, we can't keep them waiting.

I am sorry Hadassah is a little shy, but I will tell you where she is now while we wait. She lives very close to the king's palace where the colorful gardens and courts are very visible to her. The gardens are not only full of flowers and plants, but they are also surrounded by hangings of blue and white linen and there is a purple pattern on the pavement. The statues of animals and birds that are made of marble, mother-of-pearl, and other costly stones make the garden even more beautiful.

Hadassah sometimes feels like she is all alone. Her folks are dead. Her mama is dead and her daddy is dead. She does not have a sister or brother. She was very young when her parents died. She is not valued in society. The value of being a girl during this time period was very low. Fathers would sell daughters into slavery; they were considered to be a liability; they did not work on jobs; they were even sold into marriage. Being a little girl was being of no consequence: no value, distinction, importance, or purpose. Many didn't even notice Hadassah before she became Queen Esther. She was overlooked as a child.

Hadassah, where are you, girl?

Is she coming out or not?

As I said, Hadassah had neither father nor mother. Mama is dead, daddy is dead. A child can feel alone because they have no parents.

Death can mean so many different things: first, not alive but also not involved—dead, not accessible—dead, no parenting—dead, not in relationship—dead, no affection—dead, gone away—dead, nobody ever thought about what would happen to me—dead. I imagine that Hadassah like many children had a photograph in her mind of her family. The picture in the photograph is full of the colors of life: Blue cloudless skies, yellow the color of summertime forever lighting their day. Dark green, rich grass, laid out like a carpet. She and her parents share a huge, airy, white and pink cotton-candy cloud that melts because of the warmth of their dark ruby lips smiling. This photograph is only alive on paper of Hadassah's mind, because her father and mother are dead.

My work in the ministry, my career as a teacher for more than seventeen years, my work in mental health, being a mother and stepmother to five children for thirty years, a grandmother for more than eighteen years, and living the life of a young person separated from my parents have given me a firsthand look and feel for the pain of children and their behavior when they are parentless.

The story of Hadassah before she became Queen Esther offers to us a place to begin to look at and consider from the perspective of children and young people the reality of both social ills and crises that directly impact them in a most dramatic fashion. Understanding and supporting our young people's realities today will shape and ensure our future.

The children of our churches, especially those without parents, merit full partnership in the church and in the kingdom of God. Children should be considered desirable in the church. Children should not be viewed as having the type of values and needs that are not addressable in the church.

Children living without biological parents is not a new reality as Hadassah shows us. More than 75 percent of the children I have taught in Oakland have neither father nor mother. They are dead to their roles of parents and alive only to poverty, drugs, violence, crime and imprisonment. These vices and conditions have created second and third generations of children in my own family who have neither father or mother. The pain of children is real today.

I remember when I was young after my parents separated. We went to live with my aunt. We had neither father nor mother for many years. Those were difficult years for us children. I don't remember anyone in church ever talking about how to deal with our problems. Well, children and young people, since I know that you do have problems and because you matter, today I want to give some principles from the story of Esther to help you, because you matter.

1) See and admit that God has given you a family. You will find encouragement when you see and admit that the people who try to help you are not your enemies. They are on your side. I used to hate my aunt, in my own ignorance. She was on my side, she was my parent. We are told from this text that Mordecai was caring for Hadassah as if she had

been his own child, his own daughter. If God has given you somebody, accept them.

2) Honor, love, and respect those who take you as their own. We are told from the story text that Hadassah was respectful. Your attitude can take you a long way. Though she was his equal—they were cousins—yet, she honored him as her father. She obeyed him. Hadassah and Mordecai were family. Respect is a form of showing gratitude to not only the person but to God. You are saying to God, "Thank you for giving me someone to care for me." You treat these persons with love and kindness because they are God's gift to you. They are special, especially chosen to care for you by God.

3) Don't let anyone tell you you don't have any family. Some young people today don't recognize that they do have family. Hadassah just had a cousin. Some of you will say I just have my grandmother, that's family! I just have my aunt, that's family! I just have my uncle, that's family! I just have my older sister, that's family! I just have my older brother, that's family! I just have me a friend of the family, that's family! The reality of African American people in this country has never been a father, mother and two and a half children, with a house and a two-car garage. That's other people's idea of family that we don't have to fulfill to be called family.

4) Believe you have a purpose in life. God does not create junk, people do. God did not create you for nothing. You matter and were born with a purpose of God. Everyone has value and God-given purpose. Hadassah became the savior of her people! Say this right now: God created me, God is my heavenly parent, I do have a purpose! I was given life to live in this world for good. The world will be a better place because I am alive. I will fulfill my God-given purpose.

5) Believe the opportunities we have are more important than the ones we wish we had. We can trust God to weave together the events of life for our best, even though we may not be able to see the overall pattern. Hadassah did not know why her biological parents had to die. I don't know and cannot really tell you why anyone's biological parents are dead. But I can tell you that God cares and is looking to bless your lives.

Hadassah did not allow her reality to dictate her life. So many young people grow up carrying baggage like two heavy suitcases on the journey of life. One suitcase is called "what they did to me" and the other is called "what I wish I had." The baggage grows larger and heavier and all they end up doing is sharing the contents of the suitcase with anyone who will listen. Our baggage should not become our life. We were not created to examine and carry around our pain! Hallelujah!

Hadassah could have been very bitter, noncooperative, angry at life, but she chose to be a beautiful person of good countenance. Hadassah lived to realize her destiny. I don't have time in this sermon to tell her whole story, but I want you to go home and read the entire story. Then discuss it with someone close to you.

After you read the story of Esther, I hope that you will know what I know about you.

I am excited today, because of this good news for you today! You are not alone. It is time to celebrate! One of the Bible writers said: When my father and my mother forsake me, then the Lord will take me up. . . . Hallelujah! The Lord will take you up. You can trust God's word today. The Lord will take you up. Nobody can take you up like the Lord. Nobody can do you like Jesus. The Lord will take you up. The Lord God of heaven and earth cares about you! The Lord will take you up. God will be your mama! God will be your father! The Lord will take you up. God uses the people around us to show us motherly and fatherly love. The Lord will take you up.

You are loved! I know that you were created for a God-given purpose. You are special and unique. There's no one like you. No one. No one. No, no one like you! No one can do what you were created to do. I know that you are beautiful. Hallelujah! You are young, gifted, and Black. God's divine hope for the salvation of the world is wrapped up in you. God's divine hope for the salvation of the world is wrapped up in you. You do matter. You matter. You matter to the church and you matter to God! Hallelujah!

Rev. Valerie Brown-Troutt is the associate pastor of the City of Refuge Community Church, United Church of Christ, and working as the deputy executive director of the Ark of Refuge, Inc., in San Francisco, California.

"On Giving Up on People Too Soon"

Samuel D. Proctor   Acts 15:39–40; 2 Timothy 4:11

> *". . . Barnabas took Mark. . . . But Paul chose Silas . . ."* (Acts
> 15:39–40). *"Get Mark and bring him with you, for he is useful in
> my ministry"* (2 Timothy 4:11).

No one is going to live this life without some failures. It simply does
not happen that one goes from one stage of life to the next—facing the
temptations, the uncertainties, the obstacles and adversities that we all
face—without stumbling and falling somewhere along the road. Life is
made up of conditions and circumstances over which we do not have
complete control. Even when one has done the very best that one can,
when one has guarded against all error and prepared for every contin-
gency, then the unforeseen, the unexpected, the unpredictable will happen, and one will taste the bitter dregs of defeat and failure that lie at the
bottom of everyone's cup of life.

The Bible is so wonderful because it does not leave out any aspect of
human experience. Just as an artist, painting the picture of a human face,
will capture the beauty and the symmetry of that face and will also faithfully copy the moles, the wrinkles, the tiny scars, and the reflection of
the wear of the years in the corners around the eyes, so the Bible tells it
like it really is. One portion of the Bible tells of a fine young man, John
Mark, who began life with great promise but failed early.

In Acts 15 we read of the glowing success that Paul and Barnabas had
on their first missionary journey. They had preached Christ in strange
places, and the power of the Holy Spirit had followed them. They had
planted churches in strategic places and had opened up the world for
the advance of the faith. Paul and Barnabas had carried with them a
young man named John Mark. In fact, he was the nephew of Barnabas,
his sister Mary's son.

But Mark failed. In fact, he did not even finish the journey. The men
were on the first leg, preaching in the place where Mark's mother was
born and raised, when Mark quit, packed up, and went home to
Jerusalem and to his mother Mary. We do not know why he quit. Maybe
he was too young. Maybe it was too frightening traveling by foot from
one hostile town to another. Maybe he was hungry and thirsty. Maybe
he became homesick or had stomach trouble or couldn't stand Paul's

disposition or lost interest or just missed his friends back in Jerusalem. Whatever the reason, Paul didn't like it, and when Mark wanted to go on the second journey, Paul said, "No!"

This must have been embarrassing because Mark's uncle, Barnabas, was a leader in the first church in Jerusalem. He was a man of some standing. When Paul was converted on the Damascus road and nobody at headquarters believed it, Barnabas was the one man who presented Paul to the church at Jerusalem. Barnabas was *somebody*. The first church in Jerusalem had a branch in Antioch, and Barnabas was the chief preacher. He led that church for a year. He was there when the word "Christian" was first used. Pastor Barnabas was the man in charge.

When a famine swept through the Holy Land and the people in Jerusalem were without food, it was Barnabas who brought money down from Antioch to feed Peter, James, John, the brothers of Jesus, and the other believers. Barnabas was somebody special.

And Mary, his sister, was somebody, too. Remember, it was at her house that the meetings were held when the church was just starting. When Peter came out of jail for preaching, he had nowhere else to go except to the home of John Mark and Mary, headquarters for the church. Mark had a strong mother and a very highly respected and faithful uncle named Barnabas.

So, here is Mark. A young failure in life. And things could go either way with him. Would a young life be wasted? Would a career be ruined? Could he turn this failure into success? Should Paul give up on Mark? Did Mark deserve a second chance? Was Paul too hard on him? Don't we sometimes give up on people too soon? Aren't there too many persons whose lives have been unfulfilled because someone gave up on them too soon?

Of course, all of this says something about Paul also. He could lose his temper, and he was not that easy to cope with. Ask Simon Peter; he could surely tell you! From what we know about Paul, it is not surprising that some of these young men gave up on him.

We can only imagine what travel was like in those days. Maybe the food was bad, for example. Maybe there were too many mosquitoes for tent dwelling, and perhaps Paul was moving too fast. He must have had boundless energy. Without any kind of public transportation or the conveniences that we take for granted today—hot running water, rest rooms, and so on—he pressed on from one continent to another, one national capital after another, and traveled on rough seas without the kind of navigational facilities we have today. He was always living dangerously, hiking through dark mountain passes and sultry deserts. This was Paul's territory.

It had to be tough on a young man to leave home and go out with

Paul where it was hard to find fresh food, clean water, and a comfortable place to sleep. Then, with all of that, Mark was dealing with a man who did not mind going to jail every now and then! There need not be a mystery about why John Mark would be tempted to give up and go on back home.

Yet John Mark came back. What a mistake Paul would have made, giving up on John Mark too soon!

It would be wonderful to have all the details of what happened from the day that Paul fired John Mark to those lonely days that Paul spent in a Roman prison with John Mark at his side. In his letter to Timothy, Paul writes, "Only Luke is with me. Get Mark, and bring him with you, for he is useful in my ministry." And to the Colossians he writes of those who are standing by him faithfully and he mentions one Aristarchus, a fellow prisoner, and on the next breath he speaks of John Mark, nephew of Barnabas. What a mistake Paul would have made, giving up on John Mark too soon!

Reflecting on John Mark's behavior, we are reminded that young folk are in a growth process, experimenting with life, and sometimes we may be tempted to give up on them too soon. Those of us who are parents must understand this. A little reflection on our own lives also will remind us that it is not that easy! In order for young people to ripen and mature, they're going to make mistakes. John Mark faced no ordinary moral challenge. He had a great deal expected of him. He had a chance to make a mistake. He blew an opportunity and blew it badly.

Come and see that fortunately this first big blunder in life is often a temporary setback. Isn't it wonderful that most people we know lose ground for just a little while and then they make a comeback like John Mark! They find their way back sooner or later. Of course, it's always disappointing to see a beautiful life lose its footing. Tragically, this is often associated with an unsuccessful marriage or some kind of crisis in one's work. It is often the outcome of a long and clumsy wrestling with Satan and experimenting with some of life's worst moral tangents.

I'll never forget a visit I had from a very prominent citizen when I was an administrator with the Peace Corps. He said to me with one eye squinting, "You don't know me, but I know about you." He went on, without hesitation, and, in a trembling voice, he said, "I've been casting around the country trying to find a place where my young pastor can make a new start." He said someone had told him that if there was any place in the nation where people would be sympathetic and listen, it might be the Peace Corps. The Corps might help the pastor and get him on an assignment far out of the country to make a new beginning.

He said, "I love my pastor. He has spent fifteen beautiful years with us. Recently he got into sensitivity training. He began the 'touch and feel' stuff. You know pastors are under such pressure: they have to keep thinking up new things, and sometimes they go overboard with new ideas before they really understand them thoroughly. He got into this psychological 'bag,' you know, and he was training folks about how to get closer to one another. He was listening to a lot of people's secrets. Some women were freely telling about their infidelities. Young girls were telling about affairs they had had with persons of high position in town. He began to find out that a great many Christians had been 'tipping out' and having fun.

"And he said to me that in a moment of weakness he just thought he'd been missing something. Then he went on into a more serious part; he said that as he began helping these people with their problems and facing their moral dilemmas, the next thing he knew he was involved with one of them himself, and later with *another.*"

He said, "Brother Proctor, I'm telling you about a fine, God-called preacher who is in deep trouble."

He said, "I've left my work, left my desk piled up, and I'm roaming around the country trying to find a way to lift this young man out of that situation and get him a long way off so that he can get a new grip on life."

He said, "If you could find a spot somewhere in Asia, in Africa, in South America, anywhere! Get him away from where he is right now."

Bad as this situation was, and as hopeless as it appeared, here was a friend with the love of God in his heart who did not want to give up on that young man too soon!

Some of us are in unhappy situations at work; some have problems with money; and some drown ourselves in all kinds of rationalizations, and we do lose our discipline. We face these moral dilemmas, and the strength to fight the Tempter we simply can't find anymore.

> Where is that blessedness I knew
> When first I saw the Lord?
> Where is the soul-refreshing view
> Of Jesus and his word?
> Return, O holy Dove, return,
> Sweet messenger of rest!
> I hate the sins that made thee mourn
> And drove thee from my breast.[38]

Next, however, we must allow for the fact that some Christians simply never did become converted sufficiently. They loved the idea of being in church. They quoted scriptures and took Communion but never did understand the compassion of God and the love of Christ.

I have found some who lie and speak ugly to folk all the time. I know some who hate the poor, hate the weak, hate the sick, hate unpopular people, and are always seeking the friendship of "up-front" and successful persons. They brag about the "winners" they have in their circle and make clear the fact that they have no time for the "losers." And the Christ they profess spent all of his earthly days *with* the "losers" and those *farthest from* the inner circle! The kind of folk that Jesus associated with all the time are not their kind of people. They are striving to be *recognized, rewarded, honored, seen, and glorified!* Sick egotism all around us!

They dearly love the present world! They have given up on all of the things of the Spirit. They've got to have something new and dazzling all the time. The strobe lights have got to be flashing around them constantly. They are never satisfied with what they have. They are always looking for novelties, something bright with no space between delights—thrill-seeking all the time! No time for reflection about life and death, joy and sorrow, sin and forgiveness, God and his greatness, or the search for the good, the beautiful, the true, and the ultimate. None of these things appeals any longer, so they go back to "the present world" and are strong candidates for severe losses.

Finally, as a preacher of this marvelous gospel, I must affirm that God in Christ does not give up on us, not ever. The John Marks of the world are under his watchful eye. If you know anyone who has a lapse like that, if you have a lapse like that in your life, I want you to know that some of the finest names in the whole religious history that lies behind us had lapses too. Paul talked about how he had gone off the deep end, how he ran off and persecuted Christians. He could never forget standing there, watching people stone Stephen, and hearing Stephen say, "Father, forgive them. Lay not this sin to their charge." He was haunted by it, and whenever he was in deep trouble, he was happy to say, "I saw a light brighter than the noonday sun!"

So many souls have walked in the brightness of God's morning of forgiveness only after lurking in the darkness of the ugliest sins. Simon Peter led the young church, but look at how far he had to come. Jesus looked at him at that Last Supper and said, "Simon, Satan wants to sift you like wheat." Before morning Simon had lied and said he never knew Jesus.

So this is not new to us who preach. We've seen an awful lot of John Marks in our present time. And this gives us our greatest opportunity to see to it that that lapse is not a long one or a permanent one but a brief one, and that restoration is made.

This is what makes preaching so wonderful and so challenging. There are a great many John Marks out there who have not come back yet, who are wallowing in the mire of their mistakes. Nobody knows exactly what happened to them. Today it's so easy for one to get lost. The temptations are everywhere. We're drowning in pornography. The home is permeated with TV filth. Filth! They have the audacity to call them *adult* movies. It's awful when one has to qualify a movie by saying it's filthy enough now so that it's ready for adult use! What must children be thinking of "adult" tastes and requirements!

The moral standards that we learned to live by have been erased, one right after another. This is a terrible time for someone to be trying to live a life of discipline in the Spirit. Our children have so few examples to follow. They hear of important leaders lying, those in public life taking bribes, and all kinds of moral failure occurring in high places. Urban life itself allows for a certain mischievous privacy and anonymity. Grandma isn't there watching. That big, old oak tree that would speak to you if it could talk isn't there. That old backyard swing you haven't seen for a long time. Everybody we see is a stranger. This means that one is left purely on his or her own. What an awful circumstance in which to try to avoid moral collapse! Many have found it to be absolutely too much to handle.

I boarded a taxi not long ago in New York City as I headed for an engagement, and the driver said, "You look like you're in a hurry, fella." I said, "Yes, I've got to get to a church in a very few minutes." He said, "I'll see what I can do to help you."

By then he had gotten a glimpse of my face. He said, "Are you from Norfolk?" "Yes." "You went to Booker Washington High School?" "Yes." "What class were you in?" "Class of '37." "Uh-huh," he mumbled. "You have a sister? Four brothers?" "Yes." Then there was silence.

I said slowly, "Well, you must know me. Who are you?" "Well," he said, "I was in Norfolk around that time." He didn't say much after that.

When I got out to pay him, he held back his hand. "Don't pay me, DeWitt." He used my middle name! He knew me well. He then put the light on. He took off his hat as if to show some respect or to make a gesture of approval. I saw his face clearly. He *was* from our town. Then he was so handsome and clean-cut, so popular, so aspiring; but when I saw him, his eyes were bloodshot with big dark bags beneath them, and there were deep crevices in his face, marks of a rough existence.

Getting out, I leaned back into the window, and I said without thinking, "What, in the name of God, has happened to you in New York?" He put his car in gear, shut the door fast, put out the light, and sped away.

When I asked his friends later what had happened to him in New York, they said that he went up there and sank so low so fast and stayed there so long that he simply fell apart. The "world" had a hold on him.

When I see that and go into church and start preaching, I ask God to give me the right words to say and to tell me the right songs to sing and to give me the skill in preaching that can stir somebody's heart, because

I know that there is a John Mark there trying to find his way back from an awful failure.

I remember so well, as a college freshman in Virginia, high above the Appomattox River "on a lofty hill," I was trying hard to escape and to deny my rearing. I was fast forgetting Grandma and Daddy and Mamma and the Bank Street Baptist Church. I was with other freshmen trying to explore everything that the devil held before us. Then I would go to the chapel, and too often there was someone blushing to speak his name, someone afraid to talk about God in bold terms and who left me sunk down in my seat unmoved. And I was drifting farther and farther away.

But the Hound of Heaven with unhurried pace found me through this labyrinthine way. One Sunday morning—I can remember it as though it were yesterday—I got up, and I said, "I'm going to sneak off this campus. I'm going to slide down this hill and find me a church!" I didn't know which one to go to, but God sent me to the Mount Zion Baptist Church where there was a preacher who wasn't playing and who wasn't trying to talk "smart" talk.

He took a text, and he said, "As I was with Moses so I will be with thee. I will neither fail thee nor forsake thee." Then he hit me right between my eyes. He said, "Therefore, be *strong* and of *good courage.* Be not afraid, neither be dismayed, for the Lord thy God is with thee whithersoever thou goest." And he made me some strong promises in that sermon about God's unfailing love. He gave me a deal that I could not turn down.

I came out of my little seat and rushed on up there and thanked God that I believed once again that he would not fail me nor forsake me. And I kept going in the same direction from that morning on.

I didn't know what woke me up that morning. I didn't know who sent me to the Mount Zion Baptist Church. All I knew was that an angel of God must have told that preacher that I was there, a tall, skinny college freshman, drifting away from his moorings. And his words found a place in my longing heart and turned me around. Praise God!

What a privilege to know that John Mark somehow covered the distance between the day Paul fired him and that day at Rome with Paul and Peter when he wrote the first Gospel. What a good thing that Paul did not give up on him too soon!

Samuel Proctor was until his death in 1997 the pastor emeritus of Abyssinian Baptist Church in New York City, professor of the Practice of Christian Ministry at Duke Divinity School, and professor emeritus at The Graduate School of Education, Rutgers University.

Chapter 3

Evangelistic Preaching

Write as if you were dying. At the same time, assume you write for an audience consisting solely of terminal patients. That is, after all, the case. What would you begin writing if you knew you would die soon? What could you say to a dying person that would not enrage by its triviality?

Annie Dillard[1]

Introduction

*M*any have understood evangelistic preaching as central to the preacher's charge. Henry Sloane Coffin, for example, crowned it "the supreme duty of the Christian preacher."[2] But for others, such preaching calls to mind television evangelists and strident appeals for money. Thomas Long writes, "Evangelism is for many people, frankly, a nose-wrinkling word, a term they hold in approximately the same regard as the phrase 'professional wrestling.' Both are considered to be activities that draw large, uncritical crowds, involve a measure of sham, work on irrational emotions, and could end up hurting somebody."[3]

Recently, and perhaps in the face of what William Willimon calls the "We-had-better-go-out-and-get-new-members-or-we'll-die syndrome," evangelistic preaching has experienced a renaissance.[4] In this chapter, William Willimon argues that an evangelistic sermon should be faithful to the intrusive character of the Bible; Tony Campolo addresses the tension between Christ and culture; and Craig Loscalzo suggests we consider how an audience hears an evangelistic sermon.

William Willimon: Preaching as the Intrusive Word

In his book *The Intrusive Word*, Willimon remarks that if we wish to reach the strangers in our midst we must recognize "evangelism is a gracious, unmanageable, messy by-product of the intrusions of God."[5] Evangelistic preaching faithfully and boldly begins with scripture and invites God to interrupt and transform our lives.

Willimon admits, however, that his preaching has often been symptomatic of what ails preaching today: too often he has interpreted the good news as a solution to "personal problems."[6] The problem with focusing on human needs is the gospel soon becomes, in the words of Karl Barth, "an ambulance on the battlefield of life."[7] Rather than reducing the gospel to a prescription for our aches and pains, Willimon suggests we preach the complex and intrusive character of the gospel. Willimon writes that "the prime evangelistic moment [is] not in resolution and solution, but in the gap, the gap between us and God, as well as the peculiar way in which God deals with that gap in Jesus Christ."[8] To preach a faithful, evangelistic sermon we must give God ample room. "When preachers try to fill all the gaps with our suggestions for better living, or solutions to the world's problems, there is no space left for God to come and save us."[9]

To help us preach the gaps and intrusive nature of the gospel, Willimon recommends that we remember what it was like when we were strangers to the gospel. Ask yourself questions like, "How was the story told and enacted before me in such a way that I came to baptism?" "Who were the saints who modeled discipleship for me?" "When did the story of Jesus come to illumine and make sense of my story in such a way that my little life became part of the larger adventure called the gospel?"[10] If we remember how it felt to hear for the first time the scandal of the cross and the rumble of the resurrection, then we will be better able to re-create that experience for our congregation.

Willimon's approach does not ask more of the preacher, only that he or she step back and allow the gospel to take center stage. We fool ourselves and shortchange our congregations when we believe we are in control. Remember, says Willimon, when we preach we open "a package that could be charged with dynamite."[11] Trust that a congregation will respond when we explain that the Christian faith requires conversion and transformation. To preach evangelistically, charges Willimon, is to preach with a "reckless confidence in the power of the gospel."[12]

Tony Campolo: Christ and Culture

In the 1950s, H. Richard Niebuhr helpfully framed the tension between Jesus Christ and culture in five categories: "Christ Against Culture," "The Christ of Culture," "Christ Above Culture," "Christ and Culture in

Paradox," "Christ, the Transformer of Culture."[13] Niebuhr's conclusion was Christians must articulate that "in his single-minded direction toward God, Christ leads men away from the temporality and pluralism of culture."[14]

Taking his cue from Niebuhr, Tony Campolo has recently sought to address the tension between Christ and culture from college campuses to local congregations. While agreeing with Niebuhr that Christ leads us away from the "temporality and pluralism of culture," Campolo does not rush to offer Christ as the transformer of culture. As a sociologist, he argues "culture" is evolving, and in order to transform our lives we need to understand its influence. In particular, he suggests in his book *Can Mainline Denominations Make a Comeback?* that we need to understand how three "forces have overtaken traditional Christianity and made mainline churches into victims of cultural lag. These three forces are television, the emergence of the culture of narcissism, and the advent of the culture wars."[15]

The Culture of Television

While acknowledging the enormous impact television has had on how we communicate, Campolo is nonetheless skeptical of its ability to effectively communicate the gospel. He writes,

> On a large number of occasions when I have had the opportunity to address large audiences, I have taken an informal survey to see how people have come to know Jesus. I ask how many became Christians as a result of listening to some Christian radio show. Seldom does a hand go up. When I ask how many were saved though a Christian television show, the response is not much better.[16]

However, in the face of television's immense role in society, the church does need to make a decision: "Are we willing," asks Campolo, "to adapt [our] message to the configuration of a television show?"[17] Even if we say "no," the problem is "television has made the traditional religious worship experience something that seems to belong to another era."[18] In an era of rapid images and stylish presentation, church can seem boring to baby boomers or Generation Xers. Campolo maintains that while we might resist reducing our message to fit television, we do need to find ways to communicate the gospel which recognize we no longer live in the nineteenth century.

For such models, Campolo points to churches such as Willow Creek in Barrington, Illinois, which offer "seeker" services that utilize contemporary music, images and architecture. He recommends scrapping the eleven o'clock worship hour because it was "a good hour when folks had to milk cows, hook up the horse and buggy, and ride for a while to the house of God. But we are not farmers anymore."[19] An earlier hour or a service in the evening might reach more people. Finally, he wonders if in a culture of isolated individuals we might through small groups reach those people who are strangers to the gospel. In fact, Campolo shares that one Christian leader is considering using television to hook up a network of small groups scattered all over his community.

The Culture of Narcissism

The second cultural issue facing the church is what Campolo calls a "consumeristic society [which] has created a population that seeks only self-gratification."[20] Understanding that at the heart of the gospel is a call to mission and service, Campolo challenges whether the church is going to "yield to the marketplace and 'sell' a Christianity that caters to the growing self-interest of . . . narcissism, or do we . . . declare that only those who are willing to sacrificially lose themselves for the sake of Christ and his kingdom have the right to call themselves disciples?"[21]

The problem, contends Campolo, is that " 'the pursuit of happiness' is no longer just a phrase in the Declaration of Independence; it has become an American obligation," an obligation that has wound itself into our churches.[22] "For too many people," writes Campolo, "the God of love is at work in the world not so much to bring about His kingdom of justice for all, but to ensure that the individual gets all the personal happiness that he or she deserves." Christianity, of course, does not preach against happiness and wealth, but "these blessings are not our reason to exist." Therefore, an evangelistic message is at times also prophetic: "Only a prophetic church can give people what they really need. And what they really need is not what the culture has nurtured them to want."[23]

Christ and the Cultural Wars

The final cultural issue affecting our ability to preach evangelistically is what Campolo calls the "culture wars." Campolo writes, "These wars have been waiting to break out for a long time. The struggle [is] between those who believe that the Bible is a once-and-for-all revelation and those who sense a need to adapt its message to the times."[24]

The problem is that churches have allowed cultural skirmishes over politics, abortion, homosexuality, etc., to spill into their pulpits. While these issues demand discussion and dialogue, too often fundamentalist, evangelical, and liberal churches have done more harm than good by staunchly advocating one position. Campolo writes, "Personally, I think waffling on crucial issues is not the way to go. I think that integrity demands that people be true to their convictions."[25] Campolo predicts, however, if the mainline church articulates its positions pastorally and holds a middle ground, then "mainline denominational churches may be looking a lot better to a large number of people these days."[26] Our charge is to preach a balanced message. For example, "people appreciate the emphasis on personal salvation so central to evangelicalism, but [they] also appreciate the progressive social agenda promoted by traditional denominational churches."[27]

Craig Loscalzo: A New Model

Craig Loscalzo believes a new style of evangelistic preaching is needed, one that "shouts from the mountaintop that people don't have to strive to be somebody, they don't have to die of exhaustion making a name for themselves, because they are already somebody. They already have a name. They are God's children."[28] Loscalzo maintains the historical content of evangelistic sermons needs transformation from harangue to good news. In other words, evangelistic preaching should be vibrant and life-situational, embodying joy, and clearly proclaiming God's good news.[29]

Besides the tone of the sermon, Loscalzo also suggests we consider our audience. He writes, "Evangelism and proclamation begin with the assumption that some hearers, whether on a typical Sunday morning or during special services, have no biblical or theological basis for understanding any truth claims made by the gospel."[30] Do not assume, says Loscalzo, that everyone catches biblical allusions to Abraham's faith or the younger brother returning home.

But this sensitivity to the strangers in our midst does not mean we ignore or diminish our own traditions and customs. Loscalzo urges that "after all, we want them to get a feel for what it is like to be God's people."[31] Thomas G. Long adds that evangelistic preaching "is the kind of preaching which is addressed primarily to those who already trust the gospel but which, at the same time, says to those who overhear it, 'This is for you, too. The household of God is not complete until you know that you also are a son . . . a daughter. You belong here.'"[32]

And finally, and perhaps most importantly, Loscalzo reminds us that the success of our evangelistic preaching rests not with our skill, passion, theology, or rhetorical skill, but with God. "Evangelism begins with, is sustained by, and ultimately ends with God. "*We* don't convert people. *We* don't 'win' anyone to the Lord. We don't make Christians. God does. Therefore evangelism is a divine task, though it has a human dimension. We are workers *with* God."[33]

SERMONS

"A Lawyer Meets Jesus"

William A. Evertsburg   John 3:1–16

Once a man came to Jesus under cover of darkness, because his friends would have scoffed at his search for a truth they were certain he already owned. His name was Nicodemus, which in Greek means "Conqueror of the People," and that is what he was. He had scaled a lofty peak to the rarified atmosphere of leadership among first-century Jews. He was a member of the Sanhedrin; we would say he was a Congressman, a lawmaker, educated perhaps as the ancient equivalent of a modern attorney, a no-nonsense kind of guy who, as we shall see, had been trained, as lawyers always are, to pin words down to unambiguous precision, and to distrust the elusiveness of poetry, image, and metaphor.

And so in my mind's eye I see a middle-aged man in a nine-hundred-dollar suit, tastefully conservative, wingtips, and a cellular phone he has switched off, or maybe not, in order to converse in peace with the mysterious teacher he has come to quiz, for he has come to speak of nothing less than the meaning of existence.

When I think of Nicodemus, I am reminded of the lovely words with which Dante begins *The Divine Comedy:* "In the middle of the journey of our life, I came to myself in a dark wood where the straight way was lost." In the middle of his journey of life, Nicodemus came to himself in a dark wood. After a lifetime of striving, he has gained all he ever wanted, and discovered, to his horror, that it is not enough. He has the wealth of kings, the respect of all, the love of family, and the satisfaction of achievement, but he does not have God, and so he visits this new, unlettered teacher who promises a life unlike anything he has ever known. He is surprised to encounter a commoner dressed in overalls and work boots, but pays him a high compliment by calling him 'Rabbi,' a term usually reserved for scholars with several framed diplomas. No small talk, right to the deposition. "Rabbi," he says, "we can see that you come from God. Tell me something I don't already know."

And Jesus, half dodging the question, responds with an enigmatic comment that baffles the literalist lawyer. "I tell you the truth, no one can see God unless he is born from above." But Nicodemus misunderstands. As the footnote in your Bibles makes clear, the Greek preposition Jesus uses when he says "born from above" can also mean "born again," so Nicodemus, precision-driven as he is, looks puzzled and asks, "How can a man enter the womb a second time?" Remember, Nicodemus is a lawyer; he's been trained to pin words down to indisputable precision. Law school professors, and, later, clients and opponents, teach lawyers the necessity of this precision, clients and opponents like Bill Clinton: "I did not have sex with that woman," he said. Now more than ever, lawyers have learned that you have to parse every obvious, monosyllabic word in a client's sentence: "What is sex? What is 'is'? What does 'have' mean? What about 'I'? Who is that woman?" If it helps, think of the Sanhedrin as the first-century Jewish equivalent of the U.S. Senate, the lawmakers of the land, because that is what they were. Nicodemus tries to pin Jesus down to an indisputable precision. He asks, "How can a man enter the womb a second time?"

But Jesus won't be pinned down. He simply says, "You must. The once-born will always be strapped to the earth, but the twice-born, or the above-born, will know the kingdom of God."

And so this sermon is for all the apparently successful among us who've achieved all they've ever wanted, and discovered that it isn't enough. The message is: You must be born from above, or born again. I'd like to look at the experience from both angles—above and again. To put a different spin on it, the experience of the kingdom of God is a gift from above, and a process we must undergo again and again and again. A gift and a process: 'Above' 'Again.'

I. Born from Above

We must be born from above. We want to be born from below. That is, we want to lift ourselves up by our own bootstraps. We want to think that there is something we can do from below to achieve the end and goal of human existence. In Flannery O'Connor's short novel *The Violent Bear It Away,* a child tells the uncle who has raised him that he must be born again, but the uncle says, "The great dignity of man is his ability to say, 'I am born once and no more. What I can see and do for myself and my fellow man in this life is all of my portion and I'm content with it. It is enough to be a man.'"[34]

We want to think that it is enough to be a man, or a woman, that we can save ourselves by our own efforts, and find the end and meaning of human existence quite by ourselves, thank you very much. But that's not the way it works. Even to Nicodemus, even to Nicodemus, exemplar of exact rectitude, Jesus says, "You've got to start all over from the beginning and leave all your strivings and achievements behind."

Just prior to his own rebirth, Luther discovered this for himself. He beat himself to a pulp and worked himself to exhaustion and prayed himself into a frenzy and rousted his confessor out of bed at three in the morning to confess the tiniest misdemeanors, but it just was not, it seemed, what God wanted. He said to himself, "O when wilt thou at last be good, and do enough to get a gracious God?"[35] But you can't *get* a gracious God. That's what 'grace' means; it's free. Said Luther, "When we were right, God laughed at us in our rightness."[36] Jesus doesn't exactly laugh at Nicodemus, but he does tell him that the experience of God cannot be achieved by rightness, effort, or ability.

Jesus says that's as futile as managing the wind. The spirit, the breath, the wind of God is like the storms of the earth; it gales where it goes, no one can summon it, and no one can stop it. The wind has a mind of its own; it doesn't do our bidding, come when it's called, or leave when it's banished.

Just when you need it, it disappears. You're out there in the middle of the Sound hoping for a gale that will fill your spinnaker, but there's the mainsail hanging from the mast like overcooked rigatoni, and you look over to the competition's boat two hundred yards to the east and they've strapped themselves into their harnesses and the mast is keeled over thirty degrees and they're flying along at nine knots as if they had twin engines, and you think, "Those cheaters, how did they know the wind was going to be over there? Do they have a psychic aboard, or a priest?" And then, when you limp home in seventeenth place out of nineteen boats and you crank up the engine to motor into the slip, it coughs and dies, so you have to sail into the slip. Just then Hurricane Xena arrives and flings you hither and yon, and now what do you do?

Sometimes it's like that in a life with God. God doesn't do our bidding, or come when called, or leave when banished. There's nothing we can do to catapult ourselves across the chasm between heaven and earth on the momentum of our own achievement, our own knowledge, or our own goodness. "For God so loved that world that God *gave* God's only son." We've nothing to give; we can only receive.

So Jesus asks Nicodemus to start over, from above, leaving all his striving behind. He asks the successful Congressman to give himself over as a child to this new possibility. In that great book *The Varieties of Religious Experience*, William James says that there is a piano teacher who will instruct a student in some new technique, and after they've tried and tried and failed and failed, she says, "Stop trying, and it will do itself!"[37] Stop trying, and it will do itself.

Do you remember that film from a couple of years ago called *Shine*, about a piano-playing child prodigy named David Helfgott? That name is very interesting—HelfGott; is it "Help, God!"? David is trying to learn Rachmaninov's Third Piano Concerto, "The Rach 3," a piece of music as unyielding as a rock, on which many a musician has been broken. His teacher tells him that in order to feel the music, he must forget the notes, so young David does; he forgets the notes, and makes mistakes. His teacher tells him, "David, you've got to learn the notes." And he says, "I thought you told me to *forget* the notes." And the teacher says, "No, David, you've got to *learn* the notes." And David says, "Learn them and then forget them?" "Yes," says the teacher, "precisely."

It's like that with a life in God. Do you see why that musical advice is perfect for Nicodemus, exemplar of rectitude that he is? Nicodemus knows the notes. He knows the law. He's memorized most of it, and what he doesn't know he knows where to find it among the ten thousand law books that line his office, or he has three clerks or paralegals who can look it up for him. But Jesus says you've got to learn God's law, and then forget it, because the law isn't the equivalent of godliness, as Nicodemus discovered to his chagrin when he came to himself in the middle of his life. We've got to learn it and then forget it, or we'll only play the notes, and never soar into melody, because reliance on goodness is an obstacle to godliness. That's what it means to be born from above, from God, rather than born from below, of the earth. It is God's good gift, which arrests all our strivings.

II. Born Again

Or let's put that different spin on it, and look at the other possible meaning of the Greek preposition Jesus uses here: born again. Presbyterians are not terribly comfortable with this description, mostly because the corner on the 'born-again' market has been captured by evangelicals who use it to refer exclusively to those once-and-for-all experiences by which former drug addicts find new life in Jesus Christ, a radical starting-over-again by which a life is riven into two discrete halves that no longer have anything to do with each other. In evangelical parlance, before the experience, God was utterly absent from one's life, and after it, God is absolutely present, so intimate, in fact, that God's felt nearness can never be lost again.

But this doesn't happen to most Presbyterians. They never were drug addicts—how unfortunate for them—and can't turn so radically around. They've never had a day when God was totally absent from their lives, nor a day when God was so near you could see God's very face and know God's every thought. Their lives are marked not so much by this radical drivenness as by wholeness, pattern, consistency, and growth.

Elizabeth Dewberry Vaughan has written a novel entitled *Break the Heart of Me,* and the protagonist is Sylvia Grace Mullins, who is kissed for the first time by her boyfriend when she is twelve years old, but right after that first kiss, he wonders if he has done the right thing. He wonders if she is religious enough for him, and he asks her if she is born again, and Sylvia says, "I knew what he meant. I'd been at Nashville Christian Academy long enough to know exactly what he meant, and I was mad. It's not good enough to be a Christian there, you have to have a conversion experience, preferably one that makes you cry when you talk about it. You have to have a before-and-after story with big differences, like I was on drugs but now I'm clean, I was a wife abuser, but now I'm nice, I was blind, but now I see, and I didn't have anything like that. I was only twelve years old, how could I have anything like that?"[38] The rivening of life into two discrete halves may be definite for some but it is not normative for all, and to demand it of Christians who've never lived a day without God is an egregious error.

'Born again' is one of those phrases that has been taken away from intelligent Christians by its misuse among those who have had the experience. Nevertheless, Presbyterians can't just drop the language Jesus uses because some Christians have defined the experience too narrowly. Never having been a drug addict or a wife abuser doesn't preclude the necessity of starting over again. Look at Nicodemus; he was no drug addict, and God had never been entirely absent from his life. In fact, God had been very active in his life, God had been his *raison d'être*, yet Jesus demanded of him a new beginning, and so with us.

What if being born again is not a once-and-for-all, over-and-done-with experience, but a process, a lifetime, the ongoing work of discipleship? In one of his novels Robert Heinlein says that "some people seem to think that being born again is a permanent condition, like a college degree."[39] You know, once you get it, you hang the diploma on the wall, you can forget about it, no one can take it away from you, there's nothing more to think about. But what if when Jesus said to Nicodemus, "You must be born again," he didn't mean once and for all, over and done with, but "Nicodemus, you must be born again and again and again. You must always begin again in your relationship with God. When you drift into darkness far from the presence of God, you must always return to the place where the wind and spirit of God can set your sails."

Annie Dillard expresses the point beautifully. She says, "I got religion at summer camp, and prayed nightly there that God would give me a grateful heart, and received one insofar as I requested it." But then, of course, lost it again. "Inasmuch as I despised everything and everyone about me, it was taken away, and I was left with the blackened heart I had chosen instead."[40] Our own black hearts and the world's secular siren song always lure us away from God, and we must be born again and again and again, back into a life with God, or we'll be left with the blackened hearts we've chosen for ourselves instead.

E. Stanley Jones was a missionary to the Hindus and Muslims of India early in this century, and he spent a lifetime studying the conversion experience. And this is what he says: "Conversion is a gift and an achievement. It is the act of a moment and the work of a lifetime. You cannot attain salvation by discipline—it is the gift of God. But you cannot retain it without discipline."[41] That is the paradox of the born-again experience: it is a gift and an achievement, the act of a moment and the work of a lifetime. It is free, but it is costly.

A friend of mine and his wife wanted to adopt a baby and contacted several adoption agencies in the city where they lived, one of them an agency sponsored by an evangelical church, and when my friends inquired whether they would be considered candidates to become adoptive parents, the woman on the other end of the phone at the agency asked, "Are you born again?" Well, this was not the first question my friend thought he would have to answer. He was a lifelong Presbyterian and had not heard this question in a long, long time. He thought maybe he'd have to answer questions about his gainful employment or his happy marriage. He paused, for too long. He finally said, "Well, I'm a Presbyterian. Does that count?" But this was clearly not the right answer. There was a long, deafening silence at the other end of the phone, a long, long pause during which my friend felt his hope ebb away. For a minute there he thought he'd given the wrong answer and flunked the test. But the agency woman was gracious and kind and thought she'd help him out a little bit, a little hint on the exam. She said, "Let me put the question a different way. Do you accept Jesus Christ as your Lord and Savior?" He said, "Now that I can buy." That was a question he could handle. That was language he'd heard before. That's confessional language. He'd been saying that all his life, from before he could remember: "I believe in God the Father Almighty, Maker of Heaven and Earth, and in Jesus Christ, God's only begotten Son."

According to many Presbyterians, modern American religion has distorted the language of being born again by defining it too narrowly, this radical experience that cleaves a life in twain. It's too subjective, too private, too internal, and that's not something they're always comfortable brandishing about for all the world to see. But give us something objective, like confessing Jesus Christ as Lord, over and over and over again, at every juncture of life's winding path. *That* we can buy. Maybe it really is the same thing.

In his last novel, Robertson Davies talks about a literary character named Mrs. Proudie, who died of a heart attack that seems to have been brought on by self-knowledge. Slowly and reluctantly, Mrs. Proudie got wise to herself, and the knowledge was unendurable. "In the end, Mrs. Proudie died of being herself, as in the end we all do."[42] I wonder if that was happening to Nicodemus. Maybe he was dying of being himself, and he needed to be born again, or born from above, born from another power loftier and wiser than his own. Maybe in the end we all will die of being ourselves, unless the Spirit comes with power. So, if like Nicodemus you come to yourself in the middle of a dark wood or a dark night where the straight way is lost, you should come to Jesus by night, and make him Lord. Maybe you will be born again and again and again. Maybe it will not be the end, but just the beginning—of a long and astonishing journey into God.

William A. Evertsburg is the senior pastor at First Presbyterian Church, Greenwich, Connecticut.

"Yes and No"

Tony Campolo   Philippians 3:10

In Philippians 3:10, the apostle Paul prays for four things. Here they are: that we might all really know Jesus Christ. I don't mean just believe in him, but really *know* him, because there is a difference in believing in Jesus and knowing Jesus. There is a difference in knowing about Jesus and having a personal relationship with Jesus. The second thing Paul prays for is that we know Jesus, but in such a way that the power that raised Jesus up from the dead—the power of the resurrection—might be in us; because we are a weak people, we can't do much without Christ strengthening us, and yet with Christ strengthening us all things are possible.

The third thing he prays for is that we experience the fellowship of Christ's sufferings—in other words, that the things that break the heart of Jesus will break our hearts, the things that concern the Lord, the things that he feels, are the things we will feel. And lastly, this: that we might be made conformable unto his death and have the courage to carry the cross as he carried the cross and have the courage to pay the price as he paid the price, in obedience to God. These are the four things: to know him, to have his power, to enter into the fellowship of his sufferings, and to have the courage to pick up the cross and follow him wherever that might lead us.

When I pray these days, I spend a great deal of time in stillness and quiet. I don't necessarily tell God a lot of things. Oh, when I'm burdened, when I'm troubled, when I'm in pain and beaten down, I do need to talk to God and just unburden myself. But I got great news: my God knows what I need even before I ask. But the best times of prayer for me are not when I'm telling God things God already knows, but when I'm still, when I'm quiet. Jesus says if you want to pray, that's good. If you want to pray publicly, that has its reward. But if you really want to pray, go into the closet and shut the door. And so I go to the still place, or as the Celtic Christians call it, "the thin place," and be still with God. And in the stillness I let him envelop me. I let God surround me.

When was the last time you gave God five, ten, fifteen minutes of absolute silence? Where you said nothing to Jesus, but you let Jesus surround you, envelop you? If you are still with God, if you are quiet with God, if you go to the "thin place," the place where the wall between you and God is so thin, God will come through. And I call upon you, every one of you, to give God five minutes of stillness each day. Jesus did that. It says in the scripture that while it was night he would go out and be still.

Once you feel Jesus surround you, you are able to do something you are not able to do otherwise: You are able to go down deep into your heart, mind, and soul. None of us wants to explore the innermost recesses of our hearts. Many of us have just repressed ugly things. Let's be honest, there is stuff in your life that you have never dealt with. That adulterous relationship that you had years ago, that ugly thing you did that nobody knows about, that mean thing, that lie you have been living all these years. And at first you repressed them, at first they bothered you, at first they wouldn't let you sleep, but you learned to push them to the back of your consciousness, into your subconscious say the psychologists, and you think you are free from them, but you're not.

The psychologists tell us that what you have repressed still bothers you, but you don't know why you feel upset. I meet more people who say, "I don't know why I am depressed, why I am so heavy, why I am so down. There is nothing in my life that's wrong." But there were things, and you have never dealt with them because they were too ugly.

But here's the good news of the gospel. You can take the trip into the innermost recesses of your being, you can take that inner journey to the dark recesses of your mind, heart, and soul, if Jesus is holding your hand.

You need to go someplace that hasn't been visited in a long, long time and deal with stuff that you never dealt with so that you don't have to deal with it when you stand on that great day before the judgment throne. It's time to take the trip. But you can't take the trip until you know him, because the innermost recesses of your heart and mind are so filled with things so dark that you will not bear visiting them unless you are visiting them with the Jesus who forgives and cleanses.

I got a great message the other day when I went into the men's room in the airport. Now that's a strange place for God to speak to you. I closed the door. You know the door I'm talking about. And I locked it. And all kinds of things were written on the door, as you might imagine. But across it all in magic marker someone had written these words, "Judas come home. All is forgiven." What a powerful message. And it spoke to me because I believe God could forgive Judas, and you know he would if Judas went to him. You say, "He was responsible for crucifying Jesus." Well, we are all responsible for crucifying Jesus, and my gospel is I got a Jesus that could forgive Judas, and if he could forgive Judas then he could forgive me.

So don't think that you're so rotten that if Jesus takes a look at you, he will reject you if you come to him. "He will in no wise cast you out," says the scriptures.

I did an evangelistic youth crusade in Melbourne, Australia, in October this past year. It was packed out with young people. And it was an incredible service. At the end when we gave the invitation, more than twenty-five hundred kids came forward. We only had three hundred counselors, so what I did was march them out into the cricket field that was adjacent to that place. It was pouring rain, and I had those twenty-five hundred kids sit down, and I yelled, "Well, we don't have counselors, but I know what the Bible says, that the Holy Spirit is here, and the Holy Spirit will counsel you, but you have got to give him a chance, give her a chance."

So I had them still themselves and be quiet, and I said, "Jesus is around you. Now be still. And take his hand and go down deep into your heart and soul and mind and take a good look at the ugly, terrible things that you are repressing, and let Jesus absorb them into his body. As you name them he will not only forgive you but as 1 John 1:9 says, "He will cleanse you!"

And they sat there in the rain in dead silence. A half hour later no one had moved. Kids were crying and kids were changing and the Holy Spirit was altering lives. Sometimes we bring human agents to talk to people when it is the Holy Spirit that wants to talk to people.

You need to get to know Jesus. You need to take the hand of Jesus and go into the deep recesses of your being and find the forgiveness and the cleansing. When it happens, a burden will be lifted. You remember that old song, "Burdens are lifted at Calvary, Calvary, Calvary."

The second thing is that, as you find yourself cleansed, you will find yourself empowered. Let me tell you: I don't only need the forgiveness of sins, I need the empowerment of the Holy Spirit that will enable me to win victories over sin in the days that lie ahead. Don't you? I mean, I remember that story about the guy who was always coming forward, getting down on his knees at the end of the service and saying, "Fill me, Jesus. Fill me! Fill me!" Finally an old lady said, "Don't do it, God. He leaks!" Indeed, you don't need to be filled, you need to be constantly empowered by God's Spirit that will never leave you or forsake you.

In our church we had this New Year's Eve service. Remember those watch night services? And I'd be there as a twelve-year-old and couldn't wait until this thing was over. People are setting off firecrackers and yelling "Happy New Year!" and my pastor is saying, "Aren't you glad you are not out there in the world?" But I couldn't wait to get out there into the world! He said as the midnight hour approached, "Will you commit yourself to change some things in your life?" And I always would. But I was never, ever able to carry it off. And for a good reason. You might commit yourself to change, but you won't be able to because we are too weak to change. That's the bad news. You are too weak to change.

Have you ever met an alcoholic? They say, "I can stop drinking any time I want!" Have you heard that? Have you ever talked to a drug addict? "I can stop taking drugs any time I want." They stupidly think that the human will is strong enough to overcome temptation. If it was, we wouldn't need Jesus!

Jesus wants to come in and empower you to be a conqueror where you otherwise could not be a conqueror.

Some of us are so busy being phonies that we have forgotten who we really are. We are phony Christians. We walk to church, we are religious. We say all the right words.

I am always intrigued when I go to these Jesus festivals. And you go to these and everybody talks funny: Nobody talks, they "share." You don't have a good time, you have a "time of fellowship." I mean, it's so weird! And they all put on this facade of religiosity. They think that they can play the role so well that they forget who they really are.

When they made the movie *The Godfather*—which is, of course, my favorite movie—Marlon Brando, you remember, played the role of the Godfather. The movie won the acclaim of the critics, and so they had a big party. Somebody noticed that at the party Marlon Brando was ordering people around. And they said to themselves, "My goodness, he still thinks he is playing the role. He still thinks he's the Godfather."

You can play a role so long that you forget who you really are, and many of us have been playing the role of being Christians so long we forget that down deep inside we need to be dealt with. We need to be changed. And the good news of the gospel is if you get to know Jesus— if you really allow him into your life, if you take his hand and go on that long journey into the innermost recesses of your being—he will let loose within you a power that will enable you to change, and you can be more than conquerors through Christ who strengthens you.

But he will not only change you individually, he will make you into somebody who changes the world around you.

One of the most fascinating history stories I've read recently is a story of Bulgaria during World War II. Bulgaria was an ally nation to Germany. It was with Hitler from the beginning, yet this story needs to be told. Not a single Bulgarian Jew ever died in the concentration camps. And you know what did it? What did it was a man named Metropolitan Stephan, the leader of the church. When they rounded up the Jews in the capital of Sofia and put them down by the stockade near the train station and the trains pulled in to take the Jews to Auchswitz, suddenly at the end of the long boulevard leading to the train station appeared the figure of Metropolitan Stephan.

Six-foot-five to start with, but if you know anything about those Orthodox priests, they wear that thing on the top of their heads that makes them a foot taller. So he must have looked seven-foot-five. Huge white beard hanging over his white robe. And they said he walked with a stride that would amaze you. And he walked down to where the Jews were imprisoned and behind him were thousands of Christians. And they surrounded the stockade. He went up to the SS guards who tried to stop him with their guns, and he pushed the guns aside and had the audacity to laugh as he did it.

He marched into the midst of them and the Jews hysterically surrounded him, knowing they were about to be shipped to death. He raised his hands. He had the ability and courage to recite one verse of scripture. And that one verse of scripture changed the history of Bulgaria. The power of God was in him and the power of God gave him the verse. He yelled at the thousands of Jews gathered there a verse from the book of Ruth. "Whithersoever thou goest, I will go. Your people will be my people, your God will be my God." And they cheered him. And the Christians cheered. And suddenly they weren't Jews and Christians anymore, they had become one people. He changed the course of a nation.

I see change all around me in the name of Jesus. Let me introduce you to my friend Bruce. In Camden, New Jersey, he took some young people out of the Camden high school—a school where if you go there, there is a 60 percent chance that you will drop out of school. We took kids who had report cards that would amaze you, almost straight "Fs." They were reading at a fourth-grade level when we tested them. They had missed more days of school than they attended. We pulled them out of school, and Bruce set them up in groups of five. Brought in people to homeschool them. Two years later we graduated the first group of these African American young people who were hopelessly lost. And now every single one of them is registered for college in the fall. That's changing things!

We are talking about a Jesus, a Jesus who we need to know, a Jesus who will empower us, not only to be inwardly changed, but to become instruments through whom God can change people around us.

Now listen to the next phrase: "That I might know him and the power of the resurrection and the fellowship of his sufferings." Ah, people. When Jesus takes possession of you he not only makes you into a change agent, he makes you into somebody who empathizes with people who hurt, with people who suffer, with people in need.

When you look into the eyes of hungry people, you have this eerie awareness Jesus is looking back at you. And whenever you see somebody hurting, you feel Jesus hurting within them. Jesus says whenever you see somebody hungry, naked, shivering, and cold on the streets, "I am in that person." That man lying in bed dying of AIDS. What do you see when you look at him? Do you pronounce judgment? Or when you look into the eyes of that dying man, do you feel the eyes of Jesus looking back at you? For Jesus says, "Whatever you do to the least of these people, you do unto me."

Last week I was out in Colorado with a group from Columbine High School. They were all hurting, and I told them that it was right we should empathize with them. But I had to remind them of an ugly reality. That there were two boys who wandered the halls of their high school who were hurt, who were messed up, angry, and somehow we, the people of God, did not connect with those boys.

I remember the first time I went to Haiti. We have eighty-five schools for slave children there. Their families are so poor, they give their children away. I was in the marketplace and a boy came towards me begging for money. He was crippled not because he was born crippled, but because his parents had deliberately busted his arms and legs to make him into a cripple, so they can collect more money. And when I looked at that boy I saw Jesus. When Jesus comes towards you in hurting people, then in the words of Paul, we can enter into the "fellowship of his sufferings."

And then the last thing. Not only are we called to know him, not only do we pray that we have the power that was in the resurrection so we might change and become change agents, not only does Jesus create in us a loving empathy for those who hurt, for those who suffer, but Paul prays he might be made conformable unto the death of Christ. That is, he might be able to go to the garden and face the crucifixion, like Jesus did. To say "Yes!" when you have to say "Yes!" and "No!" when you have to say "No!" We need to be willing to pay the price.

Did you know why the gladiator fights stopped in the Colosseum? A young monk from France went to visit the Holy City. He got caught up in the crowd and found himself in the Colosseum. Suddenly the gladiators emerged. The young monk realized they were going to fight to the death. And from the back he yelled, "In the name of Jesus, No!" Nobody heard him. He rushed down to the barriers that separated the fans from the playing field and yelled, "In the name of Jesus, No!" But nobody paid attention. So he leapt over the wall onto the field and stood between two of the gladiators and said, "Stop! In the name of Jesus!" But the gladiators rammed their swords through him. As he fell down dead, a man in the back stood up and left. And then another and another until the place was empty. And the Emperor left and then the gladiators, and from that day the fights stopped because one man had the guts in the name of Jesus to pay the price and to stand up and to say, "No!"

There are a hundred ways you can say, "No!" When somebody at work is telling a racist joke, don't laugh; simply look into their face and say, "No!" When somebody tells a joke that diminishes a gay or lesbian person, don't laugh, but say in the name of Jesus, "No!"

Of course there are also things you have to say "yes" to. Jesus said, if you want to be my disciple, sell what you have, take up the cross, and follow me. And the rich young ruler said, "I didn't know it was going to cost that much." People, it will cost you! Are you willing to say "Yes!" when you are supposed to say "Yes!" and "No!" when you have to say "No!" Are you willing to pay the price when you have to say, "No!"

In a very small way I have had to pay the price this year. You won't believe the mail I have gotten. I don't know what's wrong. A guy calls on Labor Day from the White House and says, "My life is a mess. Will you help me?" What are you supposed to say, "I only pray with Republicans"? And I said, "Of course." And I got letters, angry letters, that said this is going to cost your ministry. And so I had to remember what Mother Teresa said when Dan Rather asked her what will happen after she dies, what will happen to the Sisters of Mercy since she was the main person who raised money. Her answer was, "It's none of my business." And that's what I have to learn. I have to learn that you do the thing that the Holy Spirit leads you to do. When somebody asks what that is going to do to your reputation, I remember I am following a man who had a lousy reputation in Jerusalem.

You gotta say "Yes!" when the time comes to say "Yes!" and you gotta say "No!" when the time comes to say "No!" Paul prays that we have the courage to pay the price when that time comes to answer. Amen.

Tony Campolo is professor of sociology at Eastern College in St. David's, Pennsylvania. Campolo has written over twenty books and has a worldwide evangelistic ministry. This sermon was preached at the Ocean Grove Auditorium in Ocean Grove, New Jersey.

Chapter 4

Topical Preaching

The sermon may or may not have a text. It must have subject.
John Broadus[1]

Introduction

Topical preaching has fallen in and out of homiletical fashion. Supporters have applauded its desire to connect with people and their issues; critics have charged that it encourages a preacher to ascend a soapbox rather than a pulpit. Henry Emerson Fosdick once grumbled that topical preachers turned

> their pulpits into platforms and their sermons into lectures, they strained after new intriguing subjects. . . . Instead of launching out from a great text they started with their own opinions on some matter of current interest, often much farther away than a good biblical text would be from the congregation's vital concerns and needs. . . . Across the years since then I have seen these topical preachers petering out and leaving the ministry.[2]

Fred Craddock has cautioned that topical preachers "have been thus lured into forgetting that they have the right to preach, not because of what they get from the newspaper but because of what they bring to it."[3]

Ronald Allen, however, has recently invited us to consider once again the strengths and hazards of topical preaching. He reminds us that, "Topical preaching is not a new idea. Honorable sermons with topical character have been a part of the church's life since its early years."[4] Some scholars have even calculated that "topical sermons have outnumbered all the rest."[5] Supporting Allen's position, Thomas G. Long remarks that, "Over the years many strong and effective sermons have been preached that were surely gospel sermons even though they were not linked explicitly to any particular passage in the Bible."[6]

In this chapter, we will examine the claim that a topical sermon is grounded in the "gospel" rather than the Bible, be given a topical preaching checklist, and look at specific topical preaching sermon models.

A Gospel or Biblical Sermon?

Allen defines a topical sermon as one in which a particular topic "calls for interpretation from the perspective of the gospel, and which can be better addressed from the standpoint of the gospel itself than from the standpoint of the exposition of a particular passage from the Bible."[7] We approach an issue from the perspective of the gospel because "the Bible is not the only guide for the Christian life. Furthermore, the Bible is silent on some subjects and can be scarcely used to address others. Occasionally the Bible is not the best guide and, in some few instances, the Bible is actually an unreliable guide."[8]

A topical sermon, therefore, is not necessarily grounded in a biblical text but seeks to be in harmony with the biblical witness. Long writes, "these sermons are really only one step removed from direct encounter with the Bible. . . . All gospel preaching, then, is in some sense biblical preaching, since biblical interpretation stands in the background even when it is absent from the foreground."[9] But what exactly is the "gospel"? Allen suggests that it is not only the life of Jesus Christ but "a working knowledge of the Christian tradition. This includes familiarity with the Bible, with the development of the witness of the church, and with current theological reflection."[10] In other words, when preaching a topical sermon Allen suggests we carry an armful of church history, theology, and biblical studies books into our study.

A Topical Sermon Checklist

To assist a preacher in preaching a topical sermon, Allen offers eighteen specific guidelines:

1) *Determine that the topic is of sufficient size for the pulpit.*
   Does the topic deal with "real life matters in which something is at stake"?[11]

2) *Identify preassociations with the topic.* "The pastor who becomes conscious of such preassociations can also become critical of them and may be able to draw upon them in the sermon itself."[12]

3) *List everything you need to know about the topic.*

4) *Search for biblical perspectives.* What other scripture passages shed light on this particular passage?

5) *Trace how the topic has been interpreted in the history of the church.*

6) *Focus on two theologians on the topic.*

7) *Bring out the denomination's position on the topic.*

8) *Investigate other relevant dimensions of the topic.*

9) *Inventory the congregation's experience with the topic.* What is a congregation's history with a topic? Their fears? Apprehensions? Joys?

10) *Imagine what it is like to be different persons in different situations relative to the topic.* "If the preacher can imagine what it is like to be a listener who is afraid of the topic, or hostile to the topic, the preacher may be able to design a homiletical approach which will not immediately push the detonator on the explosive mind of the listener but will give the listener an opportunity to consider the topic on its own terms."[13]

11) *Evaluate the topic theologically.*

12) *State your own position on the topic.* "A brief written paragraph helps the preacher develop a sharply defined position. Putting the summary of the position into writing pushes the preacher toward precision."[14]

13) *Articulate viewpoints other than your own.*

14) *Consider the mind-set and situation of the listeners in relationship to the topic.* "An experienced canoeist knows how to ride the white water so that the turbulence does not endanger the craft so much as it speeds the canoe. Much the same thing can happen in preaching; the sermon can be shaped and steered so that it takes advantage of the currents in the congregation."[15]

15) *Locate the listeners in relationship to your position on the topic.* "Step 14 gives the preacher a wide-angle view of the listeners' relationship to the topic. Step 15 is a close-up focus on the listeners' mind-set and heart-set with respect to the position the minister will advocate in the sermon."[16]

16) *State what you want to say in the sermon.*

17) *Decide what you hope will be the result of the listener's hearing of the sermon.*

18) *Design the sermon so that it will have a good chance of accomplishing its purposes.*

Preaching the Topical Sermon

As with other sermon styles, topical preaching lends itself to certain sermon designs or forms. Allen offers six models:

1) *A simple, deductive form of description, evaluation, and application.* "This form immediately orients the listener to the topic, quickly clarifies the preacher's position on the topic, provides for a description and a theological evaluation of the topic, applies the results of the evaluation to the congregation, and concludes."[17]

   Form: a. Introduction (5–15 percent)
           b. Statement of the main point of the sermon (5 percent)
           c. Description of the topic (15–25 percent)
           d. Theological evaluation of the topic (15–25 percent)
           e. Application (15–25 percent)
           f. Conclusion (5–15 percent)

2) *A structure based on the Methodist quadrilateral.* This method draws upon the Methodist theological model of utilizing scripture, tradition, experience, and reason as a guide for our Christian life. Allen writes that this form is an "especially useful vehicle for preaching on Christian doctrines. . . . The form itself systematically increases the congregation's awareness of the topic."[18] One caution is to be sure each component relates and supports the others.

   Form: a. Introduction (5–10 percent)
           b. The Bible (15–20 percent)
           c. The Tradition (15–20 percent)
           d. Experience (15–20 percent)
           e. Reason (15–20 percent)
           f. Synthesis (20–25 percent)
           g. Conclusion (5–10 percent)

3) *A model based on practical moral reasoning.* "This approach to the sermon is especially useful when the congregation faces perplexing personal and social issues. . . . [It] helps the congregation come face to face with its own

experience of the topic and with how it is affected by the topic."[19]

Form: a. The experience of the topic (10 percent)
       b. Listen to the experience of the topic (20 percent)
       c. Critical analysis (30–50 percent)
       d. Decision and strategy (20–30 percent)

4) *A general inductive movement.* "The inductive approach can be put to good use when the congregation needs to recognize and own unpleasant things about itself. The inductive homily can lead the congregation into such self-discovery, much as Nathan led David to recognize the truth about David's relationship with Bathsheba."[20]

Form: a. The preacher recounts the process of becoming aware of the topic.
       b. The preacher traces the process of discovering that the topic is also important to the congregation.
       c. The preacher "takes the congregation into the study."
       d. Using the insights that emerge from the search of the issue, what is a reasonable, Christian way for the community to understand the topic?

5) *Structure in the mode of praxis.* "The praxis approach is particularly helpful when the congregation is in a crisis of understanding or ethics. . . . The emphasis on images gives the congregation a lens through which to look at the topic, which they can carry with them."[21]

Form: a. Move one: The preacher focuses the congregation upon the specific subject matter.
       b. Move two: The preacher rereads the situation. How do we need to understand the topic?
       c. Move three: The preacher evaluates the situation and the rereading of it in light of the Christian vision and its norms.
       d. Move four: The preacher offers a new understanding or a new course of action. The preacher helps the congregation revise its patterns of thinking and living.

6) *A model that focuses on mind, heart, and will.* "This three-fold approach works best in connection with topics which are relatively uncomplicated and on which a Christian viewpoint can be established directly and without much debate. The model is especially useful for preaching on Christian doctrines. It urges the congregation to appropriate the doctrine on all levels of self."[22]

Form: a. Introduction
      b. Statement of the claim of the sermon
      c. Focus on the mind
      d. Focus on emotion
      e. Focus on the will
      f. Conclusion

Allen does not suggest we preach a topical sermon every Sunday, rather that topical preaching be seen as "a vitamin supplement to the nourishing fare of regular preaching from the Bible."[23] Allen also suggests we don't search for a topic but "let the windows of consciousness be open to the world. Needs, issues, and situations that are appropriate for topical preaching turn up in the course of living."[24]

SERMONS

"Honoring Mother and Father:
A Mother's Day Sermon"

Jon M. Walton   Scripture: Exodus 20:12

The fifth commandment is "Honor your father and your mother, so that your days may be long in the land that the Lord your God is giving you." On the face of it you would think it to be one of the easier commandments to keep. You know, honor your father and your mother. What's so hard about that? But the complexities of family life being what they are, we all know that there is good reason for this commandment to be among the ten most basic rules of responsibility in life God has given us.

Mary Pipher, in her book *The Shelter of Each Other*, describes the conflicted way in which we think of our families these days. She writes:

> (Families) are screwed up in a variety of ways. People argue or they don't express themselves, they depend on each other too much and then let each other down. Families have secrets and shame. . . . Family members ignore, control, and perpetually make mistakes. . . . We can all tell "family from hell" stories, usually about our own families. But families are also our shelter from the storm, our oldest and most precious institution, and our last great hope.[25]

On Mother's Day we are more aware than ever of the complexity of what it is to be a family today and the challenge of honoring father and mother as the commandments admonish us to do.

And maybe the beginning point is to acknowledge that Mother's Day is difficult for many people. In an article in the *Christian Century*, Mary Stimming points out the awkwardness for many who feel excluded by the festivities. Among these, she suggests, are

> . . . the couple that has buried a child or experienced a miscarriage or stillbirth; the single person who longs for a spouse and children; the woman who has undergone an abortion or placed a child for adoption; the child who has buried a mother or is witnessing a mother's illness; the mother who is alienated from her children or the child estranged from his or her mother; the

stepmother who has not yet found her place in the family or the mother not awarded parental custody. For these people, Mother's Day rituals accentuate the sense of loss.[26]

It is, after all, not easy being a parent in the first place, mother or father. It is one of the most challenging vocations God can give any of us. We have a class that is offered in my church each week called "Children Come Without Instructions," which is another way of saying that parenting comes without instructions. We learn how to be a mother or a father based on the model of our own mother or father. And psychologists tell us that in our marriages we try to replicate the spouse and marriage our parents had, except that this time we try to do it "right." And if not "right," at least our way.

The affection we were denied as children, we resolve to shower upon our children. The hugs and encouragement that crowded us or seemed too invasive, we are intent on parceling out more carefully. In truth, no one ever had a personalized manual for being a mother or a father, given the emotional baggage and personality traits and idiosyncrasies that each of us has. Inevitably we will both bless and mess up our kids somehow. It's what it is to be a human parent, and wise are the parents who get help with it when times are tough, or who at least can confess that they are not quite sure what they are doing.

In Anne Tyler's wonderful novel, *Dinner at the Homesick Restaurant*, Pearl the mother of Jenny, Ezra, and Cody—all young adults—finally hears enough of their complaints about all her faults and failings, the things she did and didn't do as a mother that are catalogued by her children. She asks if there isn't a time when the children have to live their own lives, take responsibility for their own failures, and not blame everything on her. Isn't there a statute of limitations that ever runs out on a mother's failures, she asks.

Few of us grow to adulthood and do not discover that our parents have done us no favors in some regard. If it were not so, the social workers and psychiatrists would have lost half their clientele long ago. We struggle as best we can to be good parents, and because we are human we make mistakes. We blame the innocent child for the fight that he didn't pick, we favor the youngest because she marks the end of our own youth and she always seems the most vulnerable, and while we never intended to foster the good son/bad son arrangement, what's a mother to do when one son is consistently good and the other consistently bad?

I wish we could look to the Bible for stories of hope and encouragement about motherhood and fatherhood, but all too often what we run into are the stories of disappointing families. From the first family on, Adam and Eve spawn two sons in whom there is the ultimate sibling rivalry, so strong that Cain kills Abel and so it begins. One might hope for an ideal relationship between Mary and Jesus, but from the outset it is awkward. Even Simeon, who meets Mary in the temple only days after Jesus is born, can see that because of this son a sword will pierce her soul.

When Jesus is twelve years old and is lost at the temple for three days, and Mary and Joseph—heartsick with worry for their missing son—finally find him, Jesus offers a sassy comment to his mother when she expresses her anxiety for him, "Didn't you know I would be in my father's house?" Jesus says to Mary. I don't know about your household, but in the Walton household a remark like that at age twelve would have earned me some disciplinary action!

At the wedding at Cana, when Mary tells Jesus that the wine has run out, Jesus snaps back at her, "Woman, what concern is that to you and to me?"[27] And later in his ministry, when Jesus is teaching at Capernaum, and he is told that his mother and brothers have come for him, he looks around at those whom he is teaching and says, "Who are my mother and my brothers? . . . Whoever does the will of God is my brother and sister and mother."[28] And Mary must have wondered what a strange term of endearment that might be to her.

It is not heartwarming, this relationship between Mary and Jesus. The warmest it ever gets is at the cross, when in John's gospel, Jesus tells John to comfort and take care of Mary as if she was his own mother.

It's not all one-sided. Some quite inspiring mothers are described in the scriptures. There is that touching scene, for instance, of the Levite woman who was Moses' mother in a time when the Hebrew boy-children were condemned, who put her baby in a papyrus basket among the reeds at the Nile's bank hoping that an Egyptian woman might have mercy on him and take him in. There were the two women pleading their case before Solomon, both claiming rightful motherhood, and the one who could not allow her child to be cut in two, simply to pursue her claim. And then there is probably the most tender and loving mother relationship in the Bible, which is really a mother-in-law story, the love between Ruth and Naomi, whose affection for one another was legendary, the source of the beautiful plea, "Do not press me to leave you or to turn back from following you! Where you go, I will go; Where you lodge, I will lodge; your people shall be my people, and your God my God."[29]

The biblical witness is just plain uneven in its models of motherhood. But for that matter it is uneven in its models of fatherhood, too. You know, Noah getting drunk and lying naked to his shame in front of his sons after the post-flood celebration party was no inspiring sight! Nor is Jacob showing such favoritism for Joseph over all the other children of the family, showering him with gifts and spoiling him with that enviable coat of many colors.

Probably the most likable father in the Bible to my mind is that father of the parable of the prodigal son who runs out to meet his wayward boy on the way home, but doing so in an undignified way, hiking up his tunic, running out the front door, forgetting the shame the boy has brought on the family, not even exacting a proper repentance, and leaving questions in the heart of the elder brother who has been a faithful drudge in all the lean years while the other boy was out having a big time at the casinos.

"Honor your father and your mother," the commandment tells us, and in our hearts we want to do it, like something innate. But not because there are so many inspiring models of parenthood in the scriptures. Not because in Jesus and Mary we have the definitive relationship of mother and child. We want to keep this commandment because there is something innate within us that wants to belong, that needs a place, that desires from the beginning to have arms to give us shelter, and a heartbeat to offer us security, someone who desires us and wishes us well, and who cheers us on from the balcony, and who we always hope can know us through and through and love us still and all.

And of course, few are the mothers or fathers who are so superhuman that they fulfill all we might hope our parents might be, but that we hope for them all that we do goes a long way toward our forgiving them for what they aren't. And that, it seems to me, is the essence of the commandment, know that they are not as good a mother or father as God is to us. But on earth we have no closer mediator of that divine love.

The commandment was not written, the scholars tell us, to describe the dynamic of the young child and parent, but written more for the adult child who continues to care for and love the older parent. Honor your father and mother in the years of your own parenting, the commandment seems to imply, when you reach the age they were, that your years may be blessed and that all may go well with you when you come into the promised land. This is a commandment given for those who have crossed over in their understanding, and who now know their mother and father in soul and spirit as well as their mother and father once knew them (if any of us can ever know one another that well).

There comes a time when any teenager knows that they know more than their parents know about just about everything. It is the inevitable reckoning of generations as children do what the psychologists call "individuate." We become our own person. And we realize in the process that the ones we thought had all the answers do not—that the mistakes that they make and have made are inherently human, and ones that we are likely to make as well.

The daughter who used to love to cuddle in her father's arms no longer wants his arms around her. And the son who used to love to have his ears and toes and nose and belly button kissed cannot bear the thought of his mother even giving him a kiss on the cheek within the sight of his friends.

Not until we become adults, if not parents ourselves, do we get the picture of what a difficult thing it is to be a parent. It is to have a divine responsibility with only human intellect, patience, and understanding. It's God's work entrusted to the feeble efforts of utterly human vessels, which is why the commandment is so skewed in favor of parents and so demanding of children. God has no other means on earth to do this parenting work, so we must learn to be forgiving of one another in our ineptitude.

There ought to be an equal and balancing commandment. "Mothers and fathers, honor your children that you not forget the days of your youth." But there is not. And so the burden is on the parents to know that that trust is implied.

To honor is not in essence simply to obey. It is far more involved than that. It is also to forgive, to understand that we are only human, that the one who was there at your birth and remembers the pain of the world you entered into at your arrival is but a pale human reflection of that divine love that wanted you to be here in the first place.

There are good mothers and there are bad mothers, loving mothers and spiteful mothers, freeing and manipulating, self-centered and self-sacrificing, nurturing and abusing, and all the shades and mixtures in between. And even the best of mothers know at least a few of the mistakes they have made. And some blame themselves for mistakes that were never theirs in the first place.

All of us are such mixtures of dust and glory that one brush and one color cannot catch all the hues nor suggest all the shadings. When that cord is cut that severs the connection between us and our mother at the midpoint of our bodies, it is only a physical division, and not the most important part. The emotional and spiritual ties are never broken.

And so we struggle to love and to forgive, to know and to let go, to receive and to accept the mothers and fathers of our lives, understanding that—in ways we shall never fully understand this side of heaven—God has been at work in them and in us, in the loving and beautiful things we remember of them, as well as the harsh and painful things we remember. Learning to sort and sift through those, treasuring what we can and laying aside what we must, is one of the hardest and yet most important lessons of life any of us can learn.

"Honor your father and your mother, so that your days may be long in the land that the Lord your God is giving you." Teach us, O Lord, to love, to forgive, and to honor who they were and who they are.

Jon Walton is the senior pastor at Westminster Presbyterian Church, Wilmington, Delaware. He is the author of Imperfect Peace *and was selected as one of ten "exceptional and gifted" clergy to participate in a Vanderbilt/Lilly Foundation study to attract gifted students to theological study.*

"Now That Homosexuality Is Out of the Closet, What Shall Christians Make of It?"

Ronald Allen

A. Experience of the Topic

When I was in high school in the mid-1960s, we heard very little about homosexuality. There were a few bad jokes. There were snickers when our psychology textbook reported that many adolescents go through a phase of same-sex experimentation. There was a little speculation about who might be a "fag" or "queer." But homosexuality was largely hidden. We seldom talked about it, certainly not at church.

When I was in seminary a few years later, the Metropolitan Community Church—a denomination with a particular ministry to the homosexual community—was getting under way. Several classmates were openly gay. Two women made a covenant, a lesbian marriage, in the seminary chapel. I was a twenty-three-year-old heterosexual from a conservative church in the Ozark Mountains. What was I to make of that?

Times have changed. From television characters to the local gay restaurant to gay or lesbian neighbors who buy a house together, homosexuality is out of the closet.

Even if you think this topic does not touch you, you may be surprised. How many people are gay? Estimates vary, ranging from 1 percent to 10 percent of the population of the United States.[30] Somewhere between 2.5 million and 25 million. If our congregation reflects national averages, 10 percent of the people here today may be gay. We all know gays and lesbians. Some of them are in our congregation, our circles of friends, our families.

Despite the fact that this phenomenon is more and more open, many heterosexuals and homosexuals are puzzled about the relationship of homosexuality and Christian faith. That is why we need to have a conversation as a congregation about a straightforward question. Can homosexuality be a legitimate sexual orientation for Christians?

Hearing and speaking about homosexuality have taken the edge off this reaction. I can think and talk about homosexuality in a rational way. Many people are more willing to talk about this topic today. Familiarity takes away some of the fear and anxiety.

Beyond simple anxiety, my uneasiness results from knowing that many in the Christian community are deeply divided over the subject of homosexuality. Christians sometimes explore these matters in ways that are respectful and dialogical. But we sometimes hear Christians on every side of this issue become impatient, make snide remarks, and caricature one another. Christians even shout, beat their fists on the table, and stomp out. The potential for that kind of behavior makes me very anxious.

I wouldn't be surprised if someone walked out of the sanctuary upon learning the subject of this sermon. However, I hope no one does. I hope this sermon is a part of a fair, even-tempered, and respectful conversation in our congregation in which we seek an adequate Christian understanding of homosexuality.

Some homosexual persons raise questions about their own sexuality. Is it okay to be gay? Some heterosexuals in the congregation do not know how to relate to homosexual Christians. Do we celebrate their sexuality? Do we call them to repent? Do we ignore the fact that they are sexual beings? Can the church ordain homosexuals as ministers, elders, deacons? We cannot answer all these questions in a twenty-minute sermon. But we can take some important steps.

Can loving, covenantal homosexuality be a legitimate sexual orientation for Christians? Some people answer this question with a bold "Yes." Others respond with a firm "No." Some people in each of these groups have clear reasons for their viewpoints. Other people do nothing more than reproduce hearsay and prejudice from the latest talk show. Still other people are confused by different opinions and different pieces of data: "I just don't know what to think."

B. Critical Analysis

The church interprets God's leading on specific issues by listening to the interplay of the Bible, Christian tradition, reason, and experience. What do these individual sources tell us about Christian thinking and feeling about homosexuality?

In Christian talk about homosexuality, the Bible has one of the strongest voices.[31] The way some people cite the Bible when talking about homosexuality, you can get the impression it is the only voice in the discussion, and that the Bible is filled, cover to cover, with references to homosexuality. In fact, the Bible has fewer than only five certain references.

Two passages in Leviticus forbid male homosexuality (Leviticus 18:22; 20:13). One of them prescribes a penalty for homosexuality. "If a man lies with a male as with a woman, both of them have committed an abomination; they shall be put to death."

Romans gives us a famous passage. Because of idolatry, God gave up the Gentiles to "degrading passions. Their women exchanged natural intercourse for unnatural, and in the same way also the men, giving up natural intercourse with women, were consumed with passion for one another" (Romans 1:26–27). In Paul's day, homosexual behavior usually involved an adult exploiting a child for sexual pleasure. We call that pederasty, and it may be the kind of homosexuality Paul has in mind. This text is the only passage in the Bible that unambiguously mentions female homosexuality. In this passage, homosexuality is only one of the Gentile sins of idolatry. In the end, Paul says soberly, "All have sinned" (Romans 3:23).

In a list in 1 Corinthians of people who will not be a part of the reign of God, Paul mentions male prostitutes and sodomites (1 Corinthians 6:9). Male prostitutes were boys who sold sexual favors to adults. The word translated 'sodomite' refers to a passive male in a homosexual act. This list also includes fornicators, idolaters, adulterers, the greedy, drunks, excessive partiers, and thieves. 1 Timothy mentions sodomites in a similar list (1 Timothy 1:10). If these texts provided the only basis of who would be in the reign of God, the population would be zero. Fortunately, Paul goes on: through God's grace, we can be washed, sanctified, and justified (1 Corinthians 6:11).

Those are the only definite references to homosexuality in the Bible.

A few other texts have become a part of this discussion. Some scholars think that the accounts of creation in Genesis contain implicit affirmation of heterosexuality and denial of homosexuality. God makes the woman as partner for the man (Genesis 2:18–25). This viewpoint would be consistent with attitudes towards sexuality in the eastern Mediterranean world of that time.

Some of you may be waiting for the story of Sodom (Genesis 19:1–29), from which we get the name "sodomy." Lot has angel visitors in his house. Some men from Sodom think the angels are men. The townspeople bang on the door because they want Lot to bring the visitors outside "so that we may know them." A traditional reading is that the townspeople want homosexual sex with the visitors. Lately some scholars take that passage differently. In antiquity, a community was obligated to be hospitable to visitors. From this point of view, the sin of Sodom is not homosexuality but inhospitality. I am not persuaded by the new interpretation. Nonetheless, the passage tells the story of men who want to commit homosexual rape, an act that is not acceptable in any sexual orientation.

Some people think that the reference to David loving Jonathan is a reference to a homosexual relationship (2 Samuel 1:26). I do not find that evidence convincing.

I would like for you to notice four things about the certain references to homosexuality in the Bible.

1. They are all very short. The Bible does not contain a sus-
    tained consideration of homosexuality in its complexity.
2. They all consider homosexuality in a negative light.
3. We sometimes deal selectively with the contexts of
    these passages by highlighting homosexuality and
    downplaying other aspects. Leviticus, for instance, calls
    for capital punishment for homosexuals. As far as I
    know, very few people today wish to condemn gay peo-
    ple to death.
4. There is a crucial difference between the homosexual
    actions to which the biblical texts refer and many homo-
    sexual relationships today. Many gay people today seek
    long-term, covenantal relationships of love and mutu-
    ality. None of the biblical references deal with this
    possibility.

When we turn to Christian *tradition* after the Bible, we find that, for
the most part, the Christian community has frowned on homosexuality,
believing that it violates the doctrine of creation. According to this interpretation, God intends for woman and man to become one flesh.

However, a historian at Yale University, John Boswell, finds evidence
to indicate that in practice—if not always in doctrine and legislation—
some leaders in the church and some Christian communities have
accepted homosexuality. For instance, according to Boswell, gay sexuality was "rampant" among Christians in Antioch "from the highest level
on down."[32] Prominent leaders of the church in the early Middle Ages
had a relatively indulgent attitude toward homosexuality.[33]

In the eleventh century, the gay life of a French Archbishop named
Ralph (last name) was widely known. Popular songs even circulated
about him.[34] A gay subculture flourished in the eleventh, twelfth, and
thirteenth centuries.[35]

Such cases are exceptions. Beginning with the late Middle Ages, tol-
eration for gays diminished in both the culture and the church.[36] But
there have been homosexual Christian leaders in almost every age,
including today. This slice of history demonstrates that the church has
not been of one voice in condemning homosexuality.

Inevitably we use *reason* to arrive at a conclusion. In view of the tes-
timonies of the Bible, tradition, and experience, what makes sense for
Christians to believe concerning homosexuality?[37] Reason also includes
data from the sciences such as biology, psychology, and sociology.[38] To
be honest, I am an amateur with regard to science and homosexuality.
However, I have done a lot of reading, and I generally follow those who
claim that sexual orientation is a given. But, I must admit that the scien-

tific evidence is not airtight. For instance, I recently read two articles on this subject in *Scientific American*. In one article, two scientists claim that they have found biological basis for homosexuality. They say that they have identified configurations in the brain that are slightly different in heterosexual and homosexual persons. In the very next article, another scientist challenges their conclusions.[39]

We need to pay attention to study of this matter in the physical and social sciences. But such data is relative. New data sometimes prompts us to change our minds. That may happen in the study of homosexuality. Hence, we cannot rely on this data alone.

I save *experience* for last because it seems to me to provide the most important consideration.[40] Homosexual persons say that they do not learn to be homosexual. They do not choose it. They say that their sexuality is hardwired into the self, so to speak. A noted contemporary theologian uses this analogy.

> Neither I nor any of my male heterosexual friends can recall ever having "decided" to be heterosexual. Since having fallen in love with our sixth-grade sweethearts, all we know is that we have just "been" this way. Each of us has also always been either right- or left-handed. Being right-handed is not a choice, nor a decision for which I can be held morally accountable. It is just the way I am, more like the color of my eyes, for which I am also not responsible. . . . So is my heterosexuality; it is just the way I am created.[41]

Follow this line of thinking to the next step, "If our sexuality indeed is a given, not something that we choose, then is it not one of those 'gifts' that we have from God (via whatever genetic or otherwise biological means that are yet to be determined) and hence neither something about which to boast or to refuse?"[42]

Furthermore, many gay people say that when they enter into covenantal relationships, they find stability, mutual commitment, and fulfillment. In my adult years I have known several homosexual couples who have been together for a long time. Their relationships seem to flourish and break up at about the same rates as those of our heterosexual friends.

With respect to experience, some critics of homosexuality object to flamboyant aspects of the lifestyle represented by gay bars and bathhouses. Yet, are these social institutions so different from bars where men go to meet women? A homosexual person once explained to me, "Heterosexuals have always had public places to go to meet. We've had to hide. Sometimes I'm embarrassed by the flaming displays in gay bars.

But, then, you must be embarrassed by some of the steamy things that happen in your friendly neighborhood heterosexual bars."

C. Decision and Strategy

Can homosexuality be a legitimate sexual orientation for Christians? The Bible has little to say. Five short passages. What little it says is negative. But the world of the Bible did not think of homosexuality as an orientation, nor did it envision the possibility for covenantal relationships that many homosexual people seek today. Christian tradition largely disparages homosexuality, but there are exceptions in communities that have accepted homosexuality. We can find data from the sciences that suggests that homosexuality is a part of the motherboard of the self, even if this data is not conclusive.

The experience of gay persons is the deciding factor for me. In this case, experience takes precedence over the Bible and the dominant voices in Christian tradition. Experience is also supported by some voices from the sciences.

When I have floated this way of thinking with laypeople, someone nearly always says, "But aren't you just being p.c. (politically correct)?" Well, no. The conclusion that homosexuality can be a legitimate orientation derives from an important theological corollary. God is always and everywhere present. God is always making Godself known. However, human limitations mean that we can never understand God fully. Yet, at certain times, we are more open to the divine presence and leading than at other times.

A crude analogy: Our household does not have cable television. We still receive our signal by means of an antenna. When the weather is clear and the antenna is aligned correctly, we get good reception. But when an electrical storm is in the area, or the wind changes the orientation of the antenna, the picture is fuzzy and the sound fades.

I believe that some people are more receptive to God's purposes in sexuality today than in many times past.

This way of thinking is consistent with the core of the gospel. The gospel is the news that God loves each and every person (and each and every creature) with unconditional love, and that God wills justice for each and every person in each and every situation.[43] Acceptance within the church can help homosexual persons realize more fully God's *unconditional* love. In the Christian worldview, justice is a situation in which all people are in right relationship (the relationships God intends). Homosexuals can enter covenantal relationships that God intends. Heterosexuals can relate to homosexuals with the support God wants for all in the human family.

This way of thinking is also consistent with the purpose of the church. A few years ago a significant Christian thinker described the purpose of the church as to increase the love of God and the love of neighbor.[44] The love of gay persons for God increases as they realize God's unconditional love for them. Love of neighbor increases as homosexuals more fully love one another, and as heterosexuals view homosexuals as neighbors with full standing in the human community.

This way of thinking does not give up the Bible and Christian tradition. It is consistent with covenant as the fundamental way in which God intends for people to relate with one another. It is also consistent with the fundamental purpose of sexuality in the Bible and in Christian tradition as captured in one of the frequent biblical expressions for the sexual relationship: "and they knew one another." In sex at its best, we know one another and are responsive to one another at the deepest levels. We become "one flesh." The union of one self with another self in the act of sex represents God's covenantal unity with the human family and the unity of one another in human community that God seeks for all. Plus, sex is one of God's great gifts. The pleasure that God gives through sex is a figure of the eschatological pleasure that God hopes for all. Gay and lesbian persons tell us that they can experience sex as covenantal and as anticipation of eschatological fulfillment.

Thinking of homosexuality as a possible sexual orientation for Christians is not p.c., but t.c. (theologically correct).

I do not mean to imply that every homosexual behavior is acceptable. Sexual exploitation, indiscriminate lust, infidelity, rape—such things are not acceptable in either hetero- or homosexual relationships.

One last question: "Can we trust the church if the church changes its teaching?" I reply that we change our opinions in other arenas of life in response to fresh points of view. Only a few years ago, for instance, we subscribed to Newtonian physics. But today? Quantum physics. Only a few generations ago, European American churches taught that slavery was the divine will. Only a short time ago, few congregations in the Christian Church (Disciples of Christ) had women as pastors or elders. But today, nearly every congregation has women elders. And a growing number of congregations are served by women pastors. New insight sometimes not only permits change but calls for it.

As I told you, I grew up in a setting in which we didn't talk about homosexuality. But hearing people talk about homosexuality took away some of my discomfort, and so did being around gay people. But the decisive factor is the conviction that homosexuality is the way God makes some people. I believe I have come to an enlarged view of God's providence.

I also know that this matter is still open for discussion. We are in an interim time in the church's thinking. No matter how large our view, the loaf and the cup on the Table remind us that our view is never as expansive as God's view. Divine grace makes it possible for us to continue together as a community as we think about these things. As we partake, let us receive the bread and cup as signs of assurance that God is with us in every moment of this pondering time. And may partaking be a sign of covenant with one another as we make our way towards the fuller knowledge of God in these delicate matters.

Ronald Allen is associate professor of preaching and New Testament at Christian Theological Seminary, Indianapolis, Indiana. He is the author of Interpreting the Gospel: An Introduction to Preaching *as well as many other books. This sermon embodies the structure of practical moral reasoning.*

Chapter 5

The Four Pages of the Sermon

We need a new approach to preaching, one that centers on God, one capable of fostering responsible lives filled with hope and a renewal of faith.

Paul Scott Wilson[1]

Introduction

*F*ew homileticians have ably guided a preacher from scripture passage to sermon delivery. Of those who have done their job well, *On the Preparation and Delivery of Sermons* by John Broadus held many admirers from 1870 until the 1940s, and *In the Minister's Workshop* by Halford Luccock guided pulpiteers through the 1940s and 1950s. In the 1960s many pastors favored social issues over homiletic theory, and it was only in 1971 that interest in preaching reemerged with Fred Craddock's *As One Without Authority*. It would take over a decade, however, until methods were offered that deserved the acclaim associated with Broadus or Luccock. Such books include Fred Craddock's *Preaching*, Thomas G. Long's *The Witness of Preaching*, and David Buttrick's *Homiletic*.

More recently, Paul Scott Wilson has attempted to guide a preacher through what he calls "The Four Pages of the Sermon," a process whereby the sermon is understood as four distinct sections or "pages." Each section focuses on a particular question: What is the conflict in the text? What is the conflict in the world that relates to the scriptural conflict? What is the good news in the text? And what is the good news in the world that relates to the passage? Each page has a specific role and sequence in the structure of the sermon. Wilson writes,

The four pages in sequence promise efficient and effective use of time. They help us to know what we are doing and gently steer our creative efforts in directions that are most likely to be effective for proclamation. Once we are familiar with the pages, we do not have to waste time wondering where best to put an item in the sermon.[2]

In this chapter we will examine Wilson's homiletical process as he walks a pastor through each day of the week, each day asking a preacher to accomplish a specific task.

Monday: Getting Started

After we have chosen a text, Wilson suggests we work through a short checklist to discern its theological issues and concerns.

1) *Choose a theme statement that focuses on the gracious action of God.* Wilson writes, "Preachers often miss one essential planning step that makes all the difference in the outcome of the sermon. . . . The actual starting place must be a theme statement that answers: What is God doing in or behind this text?"[3]

2) *Choose a doctrine that arises out of that theme statement.* "The sermon normally should not become an essay on the doctrine. . . . But because the doctrine offers the best reflections of the church on a particular area of thought and experience, . . . it may simply help clarify and deepen our thought."[4]

3) *Identify a need that this doctrine will meet in the congregation.* "Ask of the theme statement, 'What question does this answer in the life of a person or people in the church?'"[5]

4) *Choose one image to become dominant in the sermon.* "Use of a dominant image is essential for those preachers who tend to emphasize images and cram their sermons so full of them they are distracting."[6]

5) *Determine what mission or action of Christian service the sermon might invite.* "By mission I mean primarily one act, one action of ministry that listeners may contemplate doing as a result of the sermon."[7]

Tuesday: Page One

After working through the checklist, the next step involves locating the conflict, or "trouble." Wilson writes, "Page One is about one idea and one idea only—a theological idea about trouble in the Bible."[8] This conflict might be a disagreement between Paul and the church in Corinth or the fear the disciples felt as their boat was tossed on the Sea of Galilee. Whenever people disagree or are in physical harm or need, conflict and its outcome will keep us in suspense. But besides keeping our attention, focusing on conflict in Page One also enables us to speak pointedly about the need for and the offer of God's grace. Wilson writes, "Generally we cannot speak about God's grace without first identifying human brokenness and sin."[9]

After locating the "trouble," we then "re-create the biblical text as though it had not been heard in the first reading." To retell a text, Wilson suggests we imagine ourselves as a movie director shooting a film."[10] We might imagine, for example, "What fills the landscape as the disciples walk along the Sea of Galilee?" "What is the sound of the hammer as it pounds nails into a cross?" "What is the smell, the color of the flowers, at a wedding banquet in Cana?"

After locating the trouble and re-creating the text, we then return to our checklist and introduce our statement about what God is doing in the text, as well as our chosen doctrine, need, and dominant image.

Wednesday: Page Two

With the conflict in the text established, we then scan our lives, the life of our congregation, and the world for conflict that resonates with the conflict in the text. Wilson writes, "Page Two interprets similar trouble in the world today. In turning to this page, we span a chasm of thousands of years."[11] For example, if the trouble is that religious authorities are challenging Jesus, a trouble in the world might be that we often challenge God; or if the text reveals how Judas betrays Jesus, is our world filled with similar betrayals?[12]

Wilson suggests we look for trouble in three places: with individuals, our community, and the world. He writes,

The best preachers use vertical and horizontal trouble. . . . If we focus exclusively on individual relationships with God in Christ, we communicate an absence of God's concern for issues of injustice and suffering, and we fail to treat our neighbors as ourselves; if we focus exclusively on corporate sin and social responsibility, we ignore individual relationships before God.[13]

As we conclude Page Two, we leave the congregation longing for good news. They should be, writes Wilson, "at a place of depth, struggling with the reality of human trouble, no longer pretending that everything is okay, but ready and yearning for the help God offers."[14]

Thursday: Page Three

On the third page we set aside trouble and turn to the good news in the text. Wilson reviewed numerous sermons to locate where good news is most often placed and discovered it usually appears "only in one, perhaps the last, paragraph of the sermon."[15] The problem with leaving grace until the conclusion is, "Preachers do not demonstrate that grace arises out of the biblical text, and do not develop its impact on individual lives. Grace that is quickly dispensed is soon forgotten."[16] Wilson's method invites us to spend an equal amount of time on trouble and good news because so often, "God is missing in many of our sermons. . . . Sermons are less joyful than they ought to be. Given the good news of the gospel and all that God has accomplished on our behalf in Jesus Christ, joy seems reasonable to expect."[17]

After we have discovered the good news in the text, we once again re-create the text for our congregation. This grounds the rest of the sermon in the biblical witness and reminds the congregation our hope arises from God's activity in the text and, subsequently, in the world. "This is the only topic of Page Three," writes Wilson. "It is God's action in the biblical text."[18]

Friday: Page Four

In the last page of the sermon we build a bridge between the good news in the text and the world in which we live. "Page Four speaks about God in our world," writes Wilson. "We simply follow the promptings of the biblical text from Page Three that identified God's action in the biblical text, and now on Page Four we seek signs of that same action in the world around us."[19]

Where we look for and find those stories is crucial. "Often when preachers look for stories about God they look for stories of religious people," observes Wilson. "Such stories are good, but week by week they are hard to find and, if used exclusively, they keep God confined to the church."[20] Our examples of grace in the world should offer to a congregation a vision of how to live their lives. The breadth and scope of our illustrations demonstrating that God is active in all areas of our lives: from the boardroom to Junior League, from the cinema to the bus stop. Wilson writes,

As preachers, we provide people with a transformed vision of ordinary life that now has deep theological purpose and meaning. We are saying, in effect, the trouble is less than true, because this affirmation concerning God is true. In coming last in the sermon, grace sounds a stronger, eschatological note, the note of God's final victory.[21]

When choosing examples of God's activity in the world, Wilson also recommends we exercise care about highlighting people who accomplish deeds beyond our vision or ability. By making them examples we can intimidate a congregation. However, if we name the God who works through, for example, Mother Teresa as the same God who can work through us, then we can offer the congregation an opportunity to be empowered rather than judged.[22]

On Page Four we also review if we have woven throughout the sermon our statement of what God is doing in the text. What gives the Four Pages unity is this theme statement.[23]

An Example of a Four-Page Sermon:

The Prodigal Son in Luke 15:11–32

Page One: trouble in the Bible
The son was prodigal with his father's money
Page Two: trouble in the world
We waste what we are given
Page Three: grace in the Bible
The father is prodigal in his love
Page Four: grace in our world
God's love is enough.[24]

Law, Gospel, and the Four Pages

Wilson's model is in many ways an adaptation of Luther's counsel that we always hold up the Gospel in contrast to the Law. Richard Lischer notes that Luther understood Gospel and Law as "implacable foes," each holding forth in distinct sections of the sermon. Since Luther's time, others have unintentionally or intentionally "mixed" Gospel and Law, in particular John Wesley who saw "the law in service to the gospel."[25] Wilson agrees that law and gospel should be "mixed," but in a precise order.

While most homileticians have found Wilson's process helpful, Eugene Lowry has questioned the proportions of Wilson's method. He writes,

I disagree with Paul Scott Wilson who wants us to divide the sermon into two halves—with a "fifty-fifty balance between law and gospel." I certainly understand his concern that people carry with them from the worship service the resolution born of grace. But quantity of words is not the appropriate measure. The quality of impact, the suddenness of perception, and the power of decisive insight are central.[26]

In Wilson's defense, he does not suggest a specific percentage but that the tension between trouble and good news be accented. Wilson writes, "The goal of the four-page sermon is not to preach trouble on Pages One and Two and then erase it with grace on Pages Three and Four. . . . Rather, the purpose is to establish the tension between trouble and grace, the same tension that appropriately exists in faith."[27]

SERMONS

"When God Is Absent"

Mark Barger Elliott   Acts 1:6–14

Compared to Christmas, Easter, and even Pentecost, Ascension Sunday doesn't garner the same kind of excitement. The day Jesus was hoisted into the clouds claims none of the brass and pageantry of Easter, the banners and color of Pentecost. There are no Ascension hats at Macy's. Clergy always feel awkward with the first chapter of Acts. For how do we rouse enthusiasm for a day the disciples were left behind? How do we cheer on a day the "present Lord choose to became absent?"[28]

On this morning two thousand years ago, the disciples awoke in a good mood. They had recently peered into a damp and empty tomb, their eyes blinking in joy. Two of them strolled with Jesus to Emmaus. Thomas had stared at Jesus' nail-scarred hands. Seven disciples had passed fish with him around a charcoal fire by the Sea of Tiberias. And when Jesus had seen everybody, he told them to gather in Jerusalem and on Mount Olivet.

Now they had been on mountains before with Jesus. Peter, James, and John no doubt still remembered a cloud descending over them on Mount Horeb, Jesus transfigured into dazzling white. This time, when he appears, one of the disciples speaks right from the heart. "Lord," he asked, "Is this the time when you will restore the kingdom to Israel?"

Jesus shakes his head. "It is not for you to know the time, but you will receive the Holy Spirit and be my witnesses in Jerusalem, and in all Judea and Samaria and all the ends of the earth."

The disciple kicks a stone. I doubt this was what they wanted to hear. They had no real experience of the Holy Spirit. Pentecost was days away. Their hopes were of Elijah's chariot swooping down from heaven, crowns bestowed on their heads, the chance to sit at the left or right hand of Jesus. Perhaps they might even direct a choir of angels. And most importantly, wave to everyone who had mocked their devotion to this Galilean carpenter.

Then it happened. The text says, "As they were watching, he was lifted up, and a cloud took him out of sight."

Fred Craddock has remarked that when a parent or parents stand at the front door, baby-sitter taking off her coat, children usually ask three questions: "Where are you going?" "Can I come with you?" "When are you coming back?"

Luke tells us that after Jesus ascended two men in white robes appeared and essentially answered those very questions. "Men of Galilee," they said, "Jesus is going to heaven and, no, you can't go with him; and, no, we can't tell you *when* but he's coming back."

My son Brendan is not particularly satisfied when Lynn and I go out for an evening and promise to come back. For in the midst of saying good-bye, words carry precious little weight. As the door shuts and the child is alone, the child knows she cannot hug a promise. As Jesus sailed into the sunset, the disciples knew they could not grab an arm or a leg and pull him back down. He was gone. They were alone. The wind of the mountain flush against their face. Nowhere to go but down.

And so they wind their way down the mountain. Sliding on the gravel. I expect it was solemn. No chariots or trumpets. The present God now very absent. They were left behind, to wait.

Martin Marty, a professor at the University of Chicago, wrote a book called *The Cry of Absence* in which he reflected upon the death of his wife Elsa. After receiving hundreds of letters concerning the book, he realized that like him, many of us "have seen God excluded from their horizons."

Many of us have sat alone longing for the phone to ring. Many of us have walked into a room and remembered the laughter of a child now in college, a spouse recently departed. We have walked away from a tombstone with a lump in the throat and a hole in our heart.

Absence. The cry of absence.

Barbara Brown Taylor has observed that all of us, at one time or another, have felt that God has let us down. Maybe we prayed for a friend in middle school, a boyfriend in high school. We prayed for a parent to recover, a grandparent to be freed from pain. We did everything right, and we waited for God to answer, but the answer never came.

The cry of absence.

Who has not wondered where God was as the tragedies of Kosovo and Littleton unfolded? Could not God have descended, if only for a moment? Are not events pressing down here? Hearts broken. Lives lost.

Have we not all, at some time in our lives, climbed up Mount Olivet and asked for, even demanded, chariots and trumpets, but then lifted our chin only to feel the wind in our face and the echo of a promise told thousands of years ago?

For here we stand as Christ's disciples years later, and does it not seem reasonable to ask, what are we to do in the meantime, in this apparent absence of God?

The text says it was a Sabbath's day journey to Jerusalem. Scholars calculate this means it was about a half mile. There was time, as they walked, for someone like Peter to ask, "What now?" I would guess it took time to reach consensus. Maybe John had an idea about going to temple. Andrew thought it might do everyone good to go fishing. Peter mentioned his wife, and how they had spent so little time together recently.

But once inside the city walls Luke reveals that the disciples settled on a course of action. The text reads, "When they had entered the city, they went to the room upstairs where they were staying, Peter, and John, and James, and Andrew, Philip and Thomas, Bartholomew and Matthew, James son of Alphaeus, and Simon the Zealot, and Judas son of James. All these were constantly devoting themselves to prayer, together with certain women, including Mary the mother of Jesus. . . ."

Luke tells us the disciples, along with the others, choose two specific actions in the face of Jesus' departure: they gathered together as a community of faith, and they prayed.

I would imagine the idea caught hold when someone remembered that when Jesus was in turmoil—the press of the crowds too much, the walk to the cross overwhelming—he took time to pray. Someone else shared how they felt gathered together around the table on that Passover night, and Jesus told them from now on this bread would be his body and this cup his blood.

You see, the good news is while we wait, perhaps with a heart torn by absence, and a mind that asks, "Where is God?" the disciples remind us Jesus didn't necessarily tell us what to do in the meantime, he *showed* us.

Holly Bridges is a journalist who traveled across the country discovering what she calls "circles of prayer." She writes, "[what I found were] circle after circle of people reaching out to one another in caring and compassion, upholding one another in times of need, extending genuine love and concern. Where there is hurt, confusion, grief, anxiety, loss and illness, they are there, circles of prayer. These prayers may be petitions, silence, face-to-face, or a world away. A circle of prayer is an alliance of people who witness that we cannot walk through this life alone."[29]

In her book she tells the story of Ted and Letty Colburn, successful professionals, patrons of the arts. They have two good-looking and athletic teenagers and are members of a large suburban church. On a whim the couple decided to follow a church member's advice and join a prayer group that met every Tuesday night. About a dozen folks would come, have coffee, share what was going on in their lives, and then have a period of both meditative and spoken prayer.

Life had been going along smoothly for the Colburns until two family crises hit. First the Colburns' older son was involved in a hit-and-run accident and arrested for driving under the influence, and then within two months their younger son was caught experimenting with drugs.

The members of the prayer group recognized the Colburns were embarrassed but one said, "We wouldn't let them pull away. We knew that they couldn't get through this alone." If the Colburns missed a Tuesday night, somebody would call. Letty Colburn said, "We have been held up and carried by them. No one had done that before. They carried us through."[30]

When the disciples came down the mountain they could not have felt anything but anguish, confusion, grief, anxiety, and loss. They were probably embarrassed, wanting to return home and turn away from God. They could have locked the door of the upper room and given back the key. And yet someone remembered how Jesus had shown them how to live. They remembered in moments of crisis, Jesus turned to prayer and he turned to his disciples.

Every week in this congregation, and in congregations all over the country, we meet for worship, we gather as a family of disciples. We share the stories of our lives in a pew, before or after the service. We share the events of our lives with a cup of coffee in our hands, standing in the hall, walking to the parking lot. Some of us whisper prayers. Or squeeze hands. Or lean on a shoulder. Some of us like the Colburns meet on a Tuesday night.

I wonder if perhaps Ascension Sunday doesn't garner a lot of excitement because it speaks so pointedly to the cry of absence Martin Marty articulated so well: those moments when God feels excluded from our horizons.

But the good news is that God did not leave the disciples alone on the mountain, and he does not leave us there either. Rather, God calls us as a family of disciples to lead each other, or allow ourselves to be led, down the steep mountain trail to Jerusalem and to the upper room where we can encircle each other with prayer. And in that circle there is hope, there is strength, there is love enough to face the meantime. Thanks be to God.

Mark Barger Elliott is an associate pastor at First Presbyterian Church, Ann Arbor, Michigan.

"Calling Off Christmas"

Paul S. Wilson   Matthew 1:18–25

Sometimes the gaudy side of Christmas seems to take over. The television ad a few years ago shows a distinguished gentleman sitting at the fireside pouring his whiskey and bringing the glass to his lips, and as he tastes it, an invisible choir breaks into Handel's Hallelujah Chorus from the "Messiah." The flyer in our mailbox this week from the Humbertown Plaza lists the latest marked-down items in everything from Shopper's Drug Mart to food items at Loblaws, with the big heading, "Tidings of Comfort and Joy." When our hope is Southern Comfort and our joy is discount prices, we are in deeper trouble than we imagined. I wonder if God sometimes would like to call off Christmas, just call in sick, hang out a sign on church windows, "Closed for the season. Gone south. Back in the New Year." If you throw a party like God throws at Christmas, and you throw it open to everyone like God does, things are bound to go wrong.

In the original Christmas story found in the Bible, Joseph wanted to call off Christmas. He had been out doing his Christmas shopping. He had been shopping for a bride, looking for a partner, seeking a woman to marry, shopping for someone to call his own. He was a carpenter who worked hard from sunrise to sunset. From early morning you would hear the whine of his table saw in his carpentry shop as he worked making furniture and tools. But when he went home at night, and he closed the door, he was lonely. He was a righteous and good man. Being a good man, he took everything to God in prayer. He had turned to God, over and over. "O God, if I am to have a partner, help me to find the partner you want for me." He was not after a one-night stand. He was after a one-life stand. He wanted a partner for good, a good partner. "O God, help me to find a good woman, someone who will be a fine mother to our children and a good companion with whom to grow old." And the answer had come to him, as sure as any answer God had ever given him. "Joseph," God had said to him, "Take Mary as your partner." Joseph wasn't the only person to hear God speak. His parents heard God say the same thing. And Mary's parents heard God mention Joseph. And most important, Mary heard God. She had been doing more than a little praying on her own. When it comes to the most important decisions in your life, you want to have God's help. You do not just want to leave it up to chance. A dating service may use a personal computer, but any computer is an impersonal computer. You need something more substantial to go on, like the action of a personal God who is in control of the universe. When God sets up the blind date, when God writes out the wedding invitations, when God brings two people together in marriage, you have something solid to go on. That is what Joseph and Mary had: no less than the Word of God as their reason to wed. They were attracted to each other. They loved looking into each other's eyes. But as much as they loved each other, they loved that God wanted them to be together.

So it is understandable that when the arrangements had been made and Mary told Joseph she was now pregnant, made pregnant by God, Joseph was angry. One does not have to have a lot of things go wrong before one gets angry with God. Joseph was angry. "God," he said, "you let me down. I didn't just go anywhere when I was looking for a bride. I didn't go to a bar or a beach for a bride. I went to you. I asked you for help. I just asked for someone who was righteous and honest and truthful. Someone I could count on. And I heard you, God. You told me her name. You said 'Mary.' It's not like I misheard you. Her name starts with M. Mary does not sound like Anna, or Elizabeth, or Sarah or Ruth. You said 'Mary.' I heard 'Mary.' You said, 'Marry Mary.' And we made arrangements. We set the date. We rented the hall. We booked the caterers. Now she is pregnant? She is asking me to believe in a virgin birth—and I do not. Oh, this is a cruel trick. Have I done something to wrong you, God? Are you doing this to punish me? It's no wonder more people do not believe in you if this is how you treat them. Well, God, I want out. I can see already that this Christmas plan is not going to work. I want to call it off, the whole thing. It's a bad idea. Nothing good can come of it. It'll save a lot of people a lot of money and a lot of pain. Let's just call Christmas off."

A good many people have called off Christmas in their hearts. They may go through the motions, fetch a tree, go to parties, come to church, sing carols, give gifts, eat turkey. But Christmas has been called off in their hearts. They may love the music, and may have fond memories of Christmases past, when they set out cookies and milk for Santa, and Jesus' birth was a miracle to behold rather than a miracle to debate or dismiss. If they come to church they see the candles lit on the Advent wreath, one each Sunday through the four Sundays of Advent, and the last candle on Christmas Eve, the Christ candle, but no candle is lit in their hearts. For they have called off Christmas. They may come to church on Christmas Eve, but the church in their hearts is barricaded shut; it has no lights, the roof leaks, and the windows are broken. Only the cold north wind blows through that church, not the warm enlivening wind Who is the Holy Spirit of the living God. For Christmas has been called off in their hearts. So for them no star will shine from the heavens above Bethlehem this week, no journeying Magi will seek the birth of a King, no Mary and Joseph will look for a room, and even if they did, there would be no room in the inn of their hearts, for Christmas has been called off. The angels in heaven have been dismissed before they could sing. God's Son has been denied before he is even born, or held or beheld. Praise has been shushed before it has reached the lips. Maybe it's best to call off Christmas. Because if you let God into your heart, even just a little—even as a tiny baby named Jesus of Nazareth, a newborn infant—God is liable to take over. So call it off, say it's done. Stay safe. Stay lonely. Look out the window on a cold night where nature is stripped to the bone, and conclude that what we see around us is all there is: the skeletons of trees, icy ground, endless night. Atheism and agnosticism never saved people from a life of despair—they only condemn people to it.

I could be talking about some of our children, or some of our partners, for many of them have called off Christmas in their hearts. Is there any hope for them? But of course I am also talking about all of us, for most of us at one time or another want Christmas to be called off, if only for fleeting moments, when we do not want to be generous and do not want to reach out to others. And I am also talking about all of those people who have had Christmas called off for them, those who are seriously ill or out of work or facing layoff. What Christmas is there for the homeless? The real-live NYPD recently ordered the mobile food kitchen that serves four hundred meals a night to homeless people at Penn Central Station to stop serving. "You encourage them to gather," police said. New York City is trying to encourage its homeless people to leave town. Toronto is following New York's example. On your behalf, Deanna and members of the Outreach Committee have attended half a dozen meetings of the Coalition for Shelter in Mississauga, and recently they met with Mayor Hazel McCallion, who now seems convinced that the matter cannot simply be left to the federal and provincial governments. She has promised to work with the Coalition to solve the problem.

Does it matter that Christmas has been called off by so many people? In some ways it does not. Christmas has never been something that is up to us to perform. Christmas is something that God does. If we did nothing for Christmas, Christmas would still happen. Oh, the glamour would be gone. There would be no avenues of homes decorated with beautiful lights, no indoor trees with a star of Bethlehem on top, no Christmas cards. But there would still be Christmas. It might be much closer to the original Christmas. It would be like what happened to Joseph. He had his angry conversation with God. He had called off Christmas in his heart. He had gone to bed. But God had come to him in the night, in the form of an angel. God said to him, "Joseph. Joseph. I want to talk to you. I know that you have called off Christmas. I know you have canceled your Christmas reservations for the 'Messiah' concert. I know that you have quit my Christmas pageant. You are saying that Mary is going to have to get to Bethlehem on her own. You are not going to be the fall guy for someone else messing with Mary. Well, Joseph, that is all good and well. I do not take offense. I understand your desire to quit. Virgin birth is not an easy idea. Maybe I should have been able to come up with something better. But Joseph, there is a problem. You and I are in a relationship. We always have been. Before you were born I was in relationship with you. I called you into being. I chose you to be born. I have a purpose for your life. And I chose you to be in my Christmas pageant. And you have forgotten one thing. In this relationship of ours, we are not equal. I am the author of the pageant. You are the actor. I am the director. I give you freedom to ad lib, to say the words that seem most appropriate to you, to act the way you decide according to your best wisdom and insight, but I am the director, which makes you the directed. What I am trying to say is quite simple, Joseph. Christmas is not yours to cancel. Christmas is my coming to the earth to save my people. And I am sorry. In my pageant, you are not the star of the plot. In my pageant, you are not the fall guy taking the rap for someone else. The Baby is. In my pageant, I am taking the rap for all the sins of the world. So, Joseph, I do not want you to be concerned about what others are going to think of you. I need you to be concerned about what others will think of the Baby Jesus. He is the hope of the world, the light of lights, the bright morning star, the Word made flesh, the Ruler of all creation, the Servant King, the Savior of all who sits at my right hand. Joseph, I want you to be in my pageant." Suddenly Joseph's difficulties with the Virgin Birth faded into the background, as quickly as the angel through whom God had spoken to Joseph faded from his sight.

Today God is speaking to each one of you. "Suzanne, or Bill, or Peter, or Dianne—you have to put in your own name here—I just want you to be in my pageant. My Son is being born, and I want people to know that I am saving the world. I know that bombs have been falling in Iraq and that chaos is reigning in Washington, but I am saving the world." If we said no to Christmas, it might not be the end of the story. God might still find a way to bring the truth of Christmas into our hearts. But in saying yes, in letting our voices join the choir of angels, in making the trek to seek Jesus born in the manger, not only do the heavens resound with the glory of God, but so do all the places where we take the light of Christ, for in those places justice will reign, truth will be told, and mercy shall be as abundant as God's grace. Do you want to worship the baby Jesus this Christmas? Perform an act of kindness for someone who needs it, someone you might have ignored, and chances are, you will not be far from the one who is wrapped in swaddling clothes, lying in a manger, who comes to save the world.

Paul Scott Wilson is professor of preaching at Emmanuel College of the Toronto School of Theology. He is the author of a number of books, including The Practice of Preaching *and* Imagination of the Heart.

Chapter 6

Preaching the Literary Forms of the Bible

The preacher's task is not to replicate *the biblical text but to* regener-ate *some portion of the text.*

Thomas G. Long[1]

Introduction

*P*ublished in 1983, *Preaching Biblically* was one of the first books to focus the preacher's attention on how the form of the sermon might reflect and be shaped by the form of the biblical text. In that book, Ronald Allen writes, "The form of the biblical text and the form of preaching from that text is much like that of a building and its form. Some texts are lofty spires, others are geodesic domes, and still others are shanties. Each text has it own designs, and we live in it according to the type of space it is."[2]

Since the publication of *Preaching Biblically,* many have taken turns suggesting a preacher would do well to allow the text to draw the lines of the sermon's form. Alyce McKenzie, for example, calls this type of preaching "genre-sensitive"; preaching that recognizes a parable text quite possibly asks, and even demands, to be preached as a "parabolic" sermon. David Bartlett adds that in this style of preaching, "We want to hear sermons on Psalms that lead to song; . . . sermons on Paul that should be read like a real discussion between an exasperated Christian leader and probably equally exas-perated Christian church people."[3]

In this chapter, we will examine Thomas Long's method for approaching a text from a literary perspective and in particular how one might preach proverbs, psalms and parables.

Thomas G. Long: Moving from Text to Sermon

By the time they graduate from seminary, most students have taken a preaching class and are taught to ask a text a particular set of questions. These usually include: "Who wrote the text?" "What was the historical context?" "Why was it written?" "What is the point of the passage?" Thomas Long suggests these questions "should be augmented by questions that lead to a close analysis of the literary features in the texts and the rhetorical dynamics which are likely to take place *in front of* the texts, that is, between text and reader."[4] Long's list includes the following:

1) *What is the genre of the text?* "The Bible includes many genres: psalms, proverbs, miracle stories, parables, prophetic oracles, and short stories. . . . All of these genres embody characteristic literary patterns common to the literature of the cultures in which the Bible arose."[5]

2) *What is the rhetorical function of this genre?* ". . . discover what effect the genre of a text is likely to have on a typical reader or hearer. . . . A parable does something to a reader that a psalm does not do, and vice versa."[6]

3) *What literary devices does this genre employ to achieve its rhetorical effect?* "The previous questions asked what the text *does* for and to the reader. This question asks *how* does the text do what it does."[7]

4) *How does this text embody the characteristics and dynamics described in the previous question?* "With this question, we turn to the peculiarities of a particular text to see how *this* text, while fitting the pattern of its genre, is nonetheless unique."[8]

5) *How may the sermon, in a new setting, say and do what the text says and does in its setting?* "The preacher's task is not to replicate the text but to regenerate the impact of some portion of the text." If appropriate, the preacher might even "select for the sermon a markedly different pattern."[9]

Approaching a text from a literary perspective does not dismiss historical, liturgical, or theological questions. Rather, Long's questions seek to augment our exegetical process by discerning the "literary dynamics of the text [and] how the text guides the reading process."[10] A literary approach invites the preacher to pay close attention not only to the text, but to our particular response to the text, and how we might re-create that experience for a congregation.

Alyce McKenzie: Preaching Proverbs

Because "about the only place proverbs do not seem to be found today is in the pulpit," Alyce McKenzie believes that we must call them "forth from the tomb into a pulpit resurrection."[11] In her book *Preaching Proverbs*, she argues that it has been a mistake to dismiss Proverbs as full of contradictory advice that does not pertain to the modern world. Long adds, "To be sure, proverbs are difficult preaching texts, but to dismiss them as unfruitful is to overlook their true character and to silence a valuable voice within the chorus of faith."[12]

To preach a proverb, suggests McKenzie, we must first consider its particular literary style. A good definition of a proverb is "a short saying that expresses a complete thought, which, while most often expressing traditional values, is also capable of subverting them, offering ethical directives in certain new situations."[13] In other words, a proverb shines a spotlight onto particular areas of our lives and demands we take measure, reevaluate, and make adjustments.[14] Usually the advice it offers is blunt: Respect your parents, don't eat too much, watch your libido, care for the poor, catch your tongue.

In comparison to preaching a parable, says McKenzie, when we preach a proverb we do not re-create a story but invite a sage to speak directly as to how we are to live our lives. McKenzie writes, "Narratives seek to invite hearers and readers into a sweeping story line, seeing their lives in its story. . . . Proverbs arise out of sages' observing story lines going on around them and noting recurring patterns."[15] The patterns these sages observe usually fall into three theological categories: wisdom is a gift from God, the fear of the Lord is the beginning of the search for wisdom, and living by wisdom leads to a "certain order of personal and social life."[16]

Both Long and McKenzie stress that proverbs encourage a conversation between "common wisdom" and "biblical wisdom" and how each "inform" and shape the other. One model for preaching proverbs weaves together common wisdom and biblical wisdom by positioning a proverb throughout the sermon as if it were a chorus or refrain. Long writes, "A sermon . . . could move in just this way. Narratives, vignettes, story-like threads that the proverb tugs from the fabric of everyday life would be told, each thread punctuated by the proverb itself, quoted as an interpretive refrain."[17]

While enthusiastic about the homiletical potential of proverbs, Long and McKenzie do offer two words of caution.

1) Always "set [a proverb] within its broader canonical context."[18]
2) Set aside inappropriate proverbs such as 23:12, which reads, "Do not withhold discipline from a child; if you beat him with a rod he will not die."[19] While at times it might be necessary to discipline a child, this text clearly speaks of a type of discipline we call abusive and illegal.

Preaching the Psalms

While the psalms are considered by many as central to the devotional life, there is often a deep reluctance to preach them from the pulpit. Perhaps the reason for this is we believe a psalm is truly a hymn best incorporated into a portion of the liturgy. Or maybe we are intimidated by its poetic language, as Long writes, "to these preachers, preaching on a psalm would be like preaching on Michelangelo's *David*—too much would be lost in the translation."[20] Despite our reluctance, there are helpful suggestions on how to preach a psalm that are sensitive to its unique place within the canon.

1) *Be faithful to the imagery.* Long reminds us that "Psalms operate at the level of the imagination, often swiveling the universe on the hinges of a single image. Sermons based on psalms should also seek to work their way into the deep recesses of the hearer's imagination."[21] We make that imaginative connection when we honor and highlight the imagery in the psalm. Long writes, "Preaching the psalms, we will let the imagery be central to our enterprise, repeating the familiar, finding other images that illumine and reinforce the old."[22] Bartlett adds, "We will not need to enjoin what the psalm will induce."[23]
2) *Preach on psalms directed towards the temple.* If we are hesitant to preach the psalms because they were addressed to God as hymns, Donald Gowan reminds us that there are psalms in the Psalter that are "didactic in purpose and are addressed to human beings," for example, Psalms 1, 17, 49."[24]
3) *Build a bridge between the psalm and the congregation.* Elizabeth Achtemeier suggests we approach a psalm as any other text and ask questions such as, "What does this text mean for my people?" "How is it the mirror of their life?" "Where are they in this psalm's words?" The goal, writes

Achtemeier, is to lead the congregation "through the experience of all that the psalmist has experienced."[25]

4) *"We need not always preach on an entire text,"* writes
Achtemeier.[26] A section of the psalm may best be set aside
for another sermon, or a portion that is inappropriate for a
congregation. Achtemeier advises, however, the entire
psalm be read in worship and that we should be careful that
the "meaning of the sermon text is not distorted by lifting it
out of its context."[27]

The psalms do offer unique challenges, and yet the potential is for the
preacher to let the words of the psalms so "inspire and work among the
gathered people that Israel's stance before God becomes the congregations's stance, Israel's depth of devotion becomes their devotion, Israel's
heartfelt response to God's deeds becomes their response."[28]

Preaching Parables

Thomas Long has described a parable as a "novice preacher's dream
but often an experienced preacher's nightmare."[29] At first glance, the parables seemingly provide immediate material from which to craft a sermon.
There is often a story line with "good" and "bad" characters who embody
moral imperatives such as "forgive" or "seek the kingdom of God." But
over time, a parable's first impression often unravels, leaving the preacher
with multiple readings and approaches. On a second glance, the "good"
aren't so good after all, and the "bad" deserve a second chance. Long
writes, "As soon as we reach out to grasp a parable's seemingly obvious
truth, a trapdoor opens and we fall through to a deeper and unexpected
level of understanding."[30]

How then are we to preach a parable? In his book, *Preaching and the
Literary Forms of the Bible*, Long offers three ways to approach a parable:
as code, vessel, or object of art.

When we view a parable as a "code" we understand each aspect of the
parable as referring to a deeper, hidden meaning. The task of the preacher
is interpreting these meanings and deciphering the hidden allegory. For
example, after reading the parable of the tenants in the vineyard we might
"decode" the text and conclude the tenants represent Israel and the
beloved son is Jesus. One of the strengths of this approach, writes Long,
is by breaking the code we "confirm" the "status of the readers as insiders. Outsiders receive the literal meaning of the coded parable; only an
insider sees the fully symbolic meaning."[31] Insiders, for example, remem-

ber Israel and Jesus from previous sermons and when underscored that the parable refers to what they already know, their faith is then confirmed and strengthened.

Scholars, however, eventually came to realize not all parables are allegories waiting to be deciphered. Long writes,

> In the nineteenth century the code concept was largely replaced by an understanding of parables as vessels, that is as containers of concepts, general truths, or theological ideas. . . . Parables were no longer seen as allegories but as similes, as descriptions of everyday life which are *like* the kingdom of God in some illustrative way.[32]

The parable as vessel focuses on creating a simile rather than an allegory. It pushes us to image what something is *like* and therefore discern a previously unknown truth. The goal of the parable as vessel is discovery, not confirmation.

The third way to approach a parable is to perceive it as an "object of art." In this case the parable is unpacked as a metaphor. We do not approach an object-of-art parable, writes Long, "expecting to have what [we] already know about the kingdom of God confirmed [code] or expecting to learn something about that kingdom [vessel]. [Rather we] go expecting to be drawn into the parable and to experience the claim of the kingdom itself."[33] With the text presented as an object of art, the preacher invites the listener by an act of the imagination to wander through the parable. We re-create the experience, for example, of lying in the ditch as the Samaritan walks by, or watching a father embrace his prodigal son.

Bartlett offers three helpful suggestions on how to preach a parable as an object of art. First, allow the central metaphor to guide decisions as to what to include in the sermon. In other words, "find images or metaphors that shed enough light on the original metaphor that you can play one against another."[34] For example, if you are preaching about the treasures of the kingdom, be sure to ask what treasures the congregation has "stumbled upon this week."[35] Second, when re-creating the experience of the parable, "tell the story from one perspective." If preaching on the parable of the prodigal son, choose the perspective of either the father, the younger son, or the older son. We confuse the listener if the story is told from various points of view. Third, consider "telling the story of the parable in modern dress." "Don't do it every week," writes Bartlett, "but sometimes the retelling does make it come alive as what it is: story."[36]

While many have embraced a literary approach to preaching the parables, others question if it is theologically sound. Charles Campbell, for example, has argued that those who preach parables from a literary perspective often focus on the story to the exclusion of the storyteller. He writes, "The parables cannot be isolated from the identity of their teller, rendered in the story of his life, death and resurrection: Jesus of Nazareth defines the parables, not vice versa."[37] In other words, in our haste to decipher the deeper literary meaning we might ignore the one actually telling the parable. Dan Otto Via reminds us that,

> Jesus' parables . . . bear in a peculiar way the stamp of Jesus' mind and relate to his historical situation. . . . The parables grasp in their special way something of Jesus' ministry and make it available. . . . We in turn try to interpret Jesus' ministry in the light of his parables and, secondarily and to a lesser extent, the parables in the light of his ministry.[38]

While sermons must always be tethered to the life of Jesus, what Long and others suggest is that both the story *and* the storyteller can captivate us. The benefit of a literary approach is its desire to re-create the original intent of the storyteller. In other words, if we can discern whether Jesus drew upon an allegory, simile, or metaphor, then we can shape a similar experience for our congregation, and perhaps be faithful both to the story and to the storyteller.

SERMONS

"A View from the Ditch"[39]

David Fleer   Luke 10:25–37

The earliest experience I had with a movie of substance was *To Kill a Mockingbird*. It starred Gregory Peck. But the story in the movie was not told through Peck's character, the small-town lawyer Atticus. Rather, the tale unfolded from the memory and through the eyes of a little girl, Scout.[40] I was in grade school when I first saw the movie. While more serious than my natural tastes, I experienced the movie through the eyes of Scout, just as the movie's makers wished. I lived *To Kill a Mockingbird* through the eyes of Scout. The mysterious neighbor, Boo Radley. The fear of a frequently absent father. The terror of a dark fall evening walking home through the woods, stalked and mugged. In every scene the children are present, observing and experiencing the world around them. Do you remember how the classic movie begins? A cigar box is opened. Inside are gifts from the neighbor, Boo Radley. A pocket knife for Jem. A doll for Scout. Marbles and pennies for both. Do you remember how the story ends? Scout leads Boo, his hand in her hand, back to his home. Scout, the narrator, tells us, "Boo Radley was a good Southern neighbor who gave us many gifts, the most precious being our lives."

We viewers experienced the events, from start to finish, from the perspective of Scout and Jem. This is called point of view. Listen for the point of view in the reading of another story, found in the Gospel of Luke.

> A certain man was going down from Jerusalem to Jericho; and he fell among robbers, and they stripped him and beat him, and went off leaving him half dead. And, by chance, a certain priest was going down on that road, and when he saw him, he passed by on the other side. And, likewise a Levite also, when he came to the place and saw him, passed by on the other side. But a certain Samaritan, who was on a journey, came upon him; and when he saw him, he felt compassion, and he came to him and bandaged up his wounds, pouring oil and wine on them; and he put him on his own beast, and brought him to an inn, and he took care of him. And on the next day he took out two denarii and gave them to the innkeeper and said, "Take care of him; and whatever more you spend, when I return, I will repay you."

Everyone knows the meaning of this parable. Jesus is asked, "Who is my neighbor?" Jesus answers, "A neighbor is someone in need." The parable is set in this context where the Samaritan is an example of what it means to be a "good neighbor." That, of course, is the primary way the parable has functioned in our literary consciousness. If, however, we look at the story from the point of view of one character, we might be challenged to hear it afresh, to hear it with a new meaning for us.[41]

Every story has a point of view. Every novel. Every short story. Every movie, even *To Kill a Mockingbird*. Even "The Good Samaritan." Listen again, as if for the first time, as if you were young in your faith and were hearing these words from Jesus himself. What is his story's point of view? Where does he lead you?

"A man was going down from Jerusalem to Jericho." Who was this unnamed man? Probably, he was someone just like you and me. Like us, someone in the audience. He was from Jerusalem and he knew about this "Jericho Road." It is a dangerous road he travels, and we fear for this man. He's traveling a dangerous street. "Roll up your windows and lock the doors." This is a bad neighborhood!

About midnight a man, a forty-three-year-old preacher from the Midwest, was traveling through Detroit, took a wrong turn, detoured, lost. Road construction, flat tire. He is forced to walk the dark streets.

Whose point of view? The man on the dangerous road. This Jerusalem road is a winding and meandering road, conducive for ambushing. You start out in Jerusalem and descend twelve hundred feet to Jericho. Winding. Curving. Providing hideouts for robbers and muggers. It was so threatening that in Jesus' day, it was called the "bloody pass."

So, we're anxious for this man because we are in his shoes. Dark alleys. Dark thoughts. Then, Bam! He's mugged. Kicked. Cut. Hurt. Beat. In pain. In the ditch. One eye swollen shut. Ribs broken. Cut on the forehead.

"Help me . . . help me."

And by chance a priest passed by on the other side. . . .

"My minister . . . there he goes. Help me, brother! Help."

But he passed by on the other side.

And a Levite . . .

"An elder. One of our elders . . . Help . . . "

But he passed by on the other side.

What's wrong? Do I make them ceremonially unclean? Are they going to the temple and can't stop? Are they members of the Jericho Road Improvement Society and off to a meeting? I don't know! That's another perspective. I'm in the ditch. "Help me."

"And then a Samaritan . . . " Who? No! Not the enemy! Why, no Jew proud of his bloodline, proud of his tradition, would permit a Samaritan to touch him, let alone minister to him. Jews crossed and recrossed the Jordan to prevent going through Samaria. And, now he is here to help? No, thank you. I'll get myself out!

From the view of the victim, of the man in the ditch, the one with whom we have identified, the question of the parable is this: Who among us will permit himself to be served by a Samaritan? The answer, of course, is this: only those who cannot get themselves out of the ditch. Only the helpless. Only the victims. Only the disinherited. Only those with no choice will give themselves into the hands of their enemy.

But, I protest, "I hate the Samaritan! That phrase, 'Good Samaritan,' is an oxymoron. The Samaritan is a half-breed. The Samaritan is an alien." I protest, "The Samaritan is a friend? This is ironic. Sick irony!"

But, the parable says, mercy comes from the places we least expect. Grace is always a gift, always a surprise. That's why IRS officials and prostitutes understand the kingdom while ministers, theologians, and college professors flounder!

By itself, this story from Jesus is uncomfortable. No wonder the traditional reading focuses on the goodness of the Samaritan. The model of virtuous behavior. We've moralized the story to be able to live with it.

This parable, however, does not suggest that we put the face of a smiling man on the back of our RV and label ourselves "Good Sams." Rather, the story puts us in the ditch and says, "Now, who among us will receive the grace of God?"

My homiletical mind, probably just like yours, is uncomfortable at moments like this. My mind wanders to safe and easier stories and distant places. I race off to a battle scene. World War II. Two soldiers fighting on opposite sides. One is severely wounded. The other comes to him, cradles him in his arms, and offers him a drink from his canteen. The enemy drinks. Grace offered. Grace received.

Or, I travel south to an antebellum plantation. Master and slave. One is dying and the other carries him to receive needed medical attention. Grace offered. Grace received.

But, the madness of combat and the cruelty of slavery are easy excuses to crawl out of the ditch. No, I'm in the ditch. You are in the ditch. And the question remains, as we consider ourselves, "Who among us will allow someone we despise to be an instrument of God's grace?"

The truth is, I have people in my life from whom I do not wish to receive help. Can you think of persons in your life—races? groups? individuals?—that, if you got into trouble, you'd rather not have their help?

Beware!

I suppose that among us conservative Christians one group that we consider a threat to our children, to ourselves, to our nation, is the homosexual community. Doesn't the Bible teach about . . . them? We have good reason to be threatened by these . . . people.

Beware, lest you find yourself friendless or penniless or just can't start the car in the morning. In the ditch, and the "Good Samaritan"—or should I say, "the Good Homosexual"—finds you, feels compassion for you, comes to you, bandages your wounds, and applies medicine of friendship or finance or just a ride to the repair shop. He takes you in his car and insists to pay what you are unable to afford.

"Who among you will allow . . . ?"

For some of us, it is an individual with whom we quarrel. A despised brother-in-law. An ex-spouse. A neighbor with whom we do not speak, on the basis of principle!

Beware, lest a crisis come in your life, lest you lose a loved one, or have trouble with your children, or find yourself battling a disease. In the ditch, and the "Good Samaritan"—or should I say, "the Good Ex-Spouse"—finds you, feels compassion for you, comes to you, bandages your wounds, offers to listen to your heartache when every other decent soul passes you by on the other side. Will you allow God to use anyone, even an enemy, to be an instrument of grace? This is how God often works.

We, however, have been trained to be Good Samaritans. If I ever end up in the ditch, God forbid, please send me an older, friendlier man, driving an RV with a smiling-face, Good-Sam sticker on the rear window. Send me people I can trust, friends, family, members of the church.

At another level, a level of dis-ease, Jesus says, God's grace will be delivered by instruments of his choosing. If you accept it, without your terms, even in the form of persons you do not like, then it is grace. This is how God works!

David Fleer is the professor of religion and communications at Rochester College, Rochester Hills, Michigan. He is a member of the Church of Christ and from 1977 to 1994 served as minister for congregations in Vealmoor, Texas; Portland, Oregon; and Vancouver, Washington. He earned the M.Div. from Abilene Christian University, the D.Min. from Fuller Theological Seminary and the Ph.D. from the University of Washington.

"Welcome to the House of Life!"

Alyce McKenzie   Proverbs 9:1–6; 14:1

My Uncle Jim Fowler was one of the people in my life who taught me wisdom. He passed away five years ago. He was a United Methodist pastor in the Western North Carolina Conference, a storyteller par excellence. You could tell him a story and be sure that, when he told it back to you later, it would be much improved! He had a beautiful baritone voice and loved to sing the hymns of the Church. He loved the outdoors, loved horses. He liked nothing more than to ride the trails of the mountains of western North Carolina meditating on the beauty of the world God has made.

Uncle Jim loved the Church of Jesus Christ and poured out his energies in inviting people to its graces. He served several charges in the Western North Carolina Conference of the United Methodist Church, helped by his gracious wife Lucy. He was appointed Superintendent of Lake Junaluska, the United Methodist Assembly of the Southeastern Jurisdiction, during the turbulent 1960s. Family and close colleagues recall how the night before the vote to integrate the facilities he was prepared to surrender his credentials if the body voted against full acceptance of all God's people in God's house. After his retirement in 1976 he became, as is the habit of United Methodist ministers, busier than ever in broader church and community ministries. But he always made time for me when I visited him and Lucy at their home in High Point during my M.Div. years at Duke in the late 1970s. I was struggling with being a woman pastor in a small rural community. When some of the people came to church and saw the new Duke intern was female, I saw their backs walking out the door. "You've got to love the people of God, whether you're looking at their frontsides or their backsides," he told me. Just keep building up the household of God, and God will bless your labors in the fullness of time.

In the fullness of his lifetime, he and Lucy moved into a Quaker retirement center in Greensboro, North Carolina, first to a two-bedroom apartment. When Lucy's Alzheimer's required that she be moved to the Primary Care unit, Uncle Jim moved to a smaller, one-bedroom unit closer to her. Every night he would write her a letter and every morning walk it down the hall to her, so it would be waiting on her nightstand when she woke up. And he would spend a large part of the day sitting with her, reading her favorite poems and books to her, saying, "Oh yes, you love this one!"

Every house or apartment Uncle Jim and Aunt Lucy lived in, Jim placed his horsehead door knocker on the front door. No doorbell for him. You had to really lift this door knocker. It made no doubt all down the street or the hallway that you were there and you wanted to come in! And when you knocked, his cheerful, resonant voice would sound from within: "Come in the House!"

This is Welcome Mat Sunday. This is "Come in the House!" Sunday. Some of you have been away and are back. Some of you may be here for the first time. Whichever you are, we all like a warm welcome.

For hospitality nothing in the Bible beats the description of Woman Wisdom in chapter 9 of Proverbs. There's nothing more annoying than putting dinner on the table, calling everyone, and having nobody come. Picture Mama standing on the doorstep at supper time, teatowel over her arm, demanding, "It's about time! Where have you been? Get in this house! Wash those hands. Supper's ready!"

"Wisdom has built her house, she has hewn her seven pillars. She has slaughtered her animals, she has mixed her wine, she has also set her table. She has sent out her servant-girls, she calls from the highest places in the town, 'You that are simple, turn in here!' To those without sense she says, 'Come, eat of my bread and drink of the wine I have mixed. Lay aside immaturity, and live, and walk in the way of insight.'" (Proverbs 9:1–6)

Woman Wisdom models inclusive hospitality—how to give a warm welcome—and she serves up some free advice along with the home-cooked meal. "The wise woman builds her house, but the foolish tears it down with her own hands." (14:1)

What kind of house is it we are to build? I've just moved to Texas from Pennsylvania, which you may know means "Penn's Woods." With its lush, tree-covered hills it lives up to its name. Now Texas has a beauty of its own, but I've noticed there is a bit of wishful thinking going on in the names they give to streets here: ForestGlen, Shadetree Lane. Then there's my personal favorite, Rainforest Drive. We name our streets for what we wish our surroundings were. And what they may one day be. The trees will grow and maybe in fifty years, the name Shadetree Lane will fit. With wishful thinking we name our Church. We gathered here this morning call ourselves the Church of Jesus Christ. Yes and no, not yet. Woman Wisdom, whose teachings and invitation inspired those of Jesus, would embolden us to call the Church the Household of Wisdom! Or the House of Life!

The Ancient Egyptian teachers of wisdom, whose teachings influenced those of Israel, called the schools the House of Life. The House of

Life was part library, part classroom, and part place of worship. Wise teachers trained young students to become 'scribes of the House of Life.'

The Church has been compared with many things through the centuries: a hospital for sinners, the bride of Christ, the ark of salvation, the defender and preserver of the faith. Why not add this biblical image of the Church as the House of Life: where we learn and teach wisdom and worship its Creator!

But the Church isn't the only House of Life. In Israel wisdom education occurred in temple and court, but also and even earlier, by the hearth, in the fields. Next to my son's fifth-grade classroom a laminated sign says, "A classroom is four walls filled with hope." That's what a House of Life is.

Those are the kinds of houses Woman Wisdom likes to build. She is the housebuilder of creation with God in Proverbs 8. In a lyrical passage from The Wisdom of Solomon 6:12–16, Wisdom is depicted as waiting at the entrance to one's house, waiting to be invited in. Proverbs 14:33 tells us that "Wisdom is at home in the mind of one who has understanding, but it is not known in the heart of fools." Wisdom is always looking for a room. "Foxes have holes, and the birds of the air have nests, but the Son of Man has nowhere to lay his head."

The House of Wisdom or Life is this world, your heart, all the places where this week you learn and teach wisdom and give glory to its Creator. Not every House of Life smells like incense, candle wax, and lemon oil. Some smell like musty books, some like aging bodies, some like popcorn, some like fresh paint. It is your four walls filled with hope.

Of course, not all four walls are filled with hope. My sister is a counselor for a domestic-abuse clinic in rural Central Pennsylvania. Were she here, she would tell you what you may have already experienced, that not all houses are four walls filled with hope.

Not all churches are four walls filled with hope. I've known churches that are more like the House of Usher than a House of Life. Places where people tear down rather than build up. A proverb from New England says, "It takes a carpenter to build a barn, but any donkey can kick one down." Sometimes we are both carpenter and donkey.

A foolish person tears down what she has built with her own two hands. I have a friend who was attending a professional meeting where people go to build relationships and learn from each other's cutting-edge scholarship. They had for sale all the books by the members displayed on tables. He and I were both graduate students at the time, eager to meet and greet, to see and be seen by the big lights in the field. I walked up to him and saw that he was looking at a new book on a topic of mutual interest to us. "This looks interesting," I said. "It's about time our field had a full-blown treatment of this." "Well," he said, "it wouldn't be my pick. I don't see anything in it that hasn't been said before." I moved on down the table without making any comment. Mercifully so. Because as I moved on, I saw out of the corner of my eye a bearded man who had been standing behind us tap my friend on the shoulder and shake his hand, saying, "I'm the author. So you thought my constructive concluding chapter was purely derivative?" I saw my friend blanch, because he hadn't read the book. I broke into a cold sweat of vicarious empathy, thinking "There but by the grace of God go I." Criticizing without full knowledge is one of our favorite indoor sports— whether in the church, school, office, or nation.

Our society is good at building prisons, not so good at assuring every schoolchild access to textbooks, adequate supplies, teachers, and a computer. We are good at building middle-class children who know technology and know how to compete on the athletic field, good traits to become competitive consumers, but how are we teaching them wisdom? A wise woman builds her house!

One of my favorite cartoons depicts a man standing in line at the pearly gates. St. Peter looms over him. The man is wearing a T-shirt on which is inscribed a common saying these days, the polite version of which is "stuff happens." He has his hand raised and is asking, "Please, may I go home first and change my shirt?"

A common saying among Egyptian wisdom teachers was "No one is born wise." Nor does the flipping of calendar pages guarantee that we die wise. In between cradle and grave, we have a House of Life to build.

We have an invitation to accept to fear God and seek wisdom: to leave behind envy and vicious speech and bad habits and indifference to those on the margins. We have an invitation to extend to a society filled with the spiritually homeless. A woman once told her pastor about her first Sunday coming to church. She cowered behind a pillar in the narthex like a deer in the headlights, unsure she was dressed appropriately, looking in and seeing that lots of people didn't even need to look at their hymnals to know the words. Maybe you've been or are that person this morning. Maybe you're one of the hymn singers who needs to turn around and say, "It doesn't matter where you've been, how you're dressed, or whether you know the words. Come in the house!"

Recently Dorothy Burse Holmes, longtime educator in the Dallas public schools, first lady of St. Luke's Community United Methodist Church, and wife of its Pastor Zan Holmes, passed away. I never had the privilege of meeting Dorothy, but I attended her funeral service, and there, through the stories of those whose lives she had touched, I met Dorothy. One of those people was Rickie Rush, now the pastor of The Inspiring Body Church of Christ in Dallas. Rickie told how when he was in the fourth grade, he went to school the first day and his teacher was a beautiful woman with glowing eyes and a kind smile. He fell in love on the spot. He came home from school and told his mother jubilantly, "Momma, guess what? My new teacher is Lena Horne!" Mrs. Holmes ran a tight ship. She didn't hold with her students staying home pretending they were sick or coming to class with undone homework. But he loved her still.

Halfway through the year, Rickie's mother died. The family all came to the funeral, then went their separate ways, and somehow, in all the confusion, this ten-year-old boy was left alone in the apartment. For a day and a night and into the next day. "I was afraid," he said. "I was alone. I was on the verge of panic." Then, looking out his window, he saw her—striding up the path to his door, and she didn't look entirely happy. She was coming to find out why her student was not in school.

"I was alone. I was afraid. I was on the verge of panic, but she took me home!" And over the years, though he lived with others, she saw to it that he had care and school clothes and school supplies, and did I mention care?

I feel sure that when Uncle Jim and Dorothy Holmes made the passage to the next life and stood at that new portal, they heard a warm and welcoming voice calling out to them from within, "Come in the House!" By the grace of God we experience in Jesus Christ our Lord, let us both accept and extend that invitation.

Alyce M. McKenzie is assistant professor of homiletics at Perkins School of Theology in Dallas, Texas, and the author of Preaching Proverbs: Wisdom for the Pulpit *and* Interpretation Bible Studies: Matthew, *as well as numerous articles that have appeared in various journals relating to preaching.*

Chapter 7

Pastoral Preaching

So, why not think of the sermon, instead of as a public utter-
ance, as something you are saying to somebody you love, to
your best friend?

Frederick Buechner[1]

Introduction

*I*n Thomas Long's book *The Witness of Preaching,* four images are
identified to suggest how a preacher might best approach the task of
preaching. The first image is the *herald* who seeks not to bestow
advice, express opinions, or sparkle with personality, but is a faithful messenger through which the word of God flows. The second
image is the *storyteller* who weaves the narrative of the biblical story
with the narrative of our lives. The third image is the *witness* who
approaches the text patiently, waiting to encounter a word from the
Lord and then return and testify to the congregation what "has been
seen and heard through the scripture."[2]

The fourth image Long describes is the *pastor.* Here the preacher
"seeks to enable some beneficial change in the hearers, attempts to
help them make sense of their lives, and strives to be a catalyst for
more responsible living on the part of those who hear."[3] A pastoral
preacher, in other words, begins with the issues of the congregation
clearly in mind. Henry Emerson Fosdick, a strong proponent of such
preaching, wrote, "We need more sermons that try to face people's
real problems with them, meet their difficulties, answer their questions, confirm their noblest faiths and interpret their experiences in
sympathetic, wise, and understanding co-operation."[4] Fosdick
believed the key to preaching effectively was understanding that

preaching and personal counseling went hand in hand. William Willimon writes, "The leader of the liturgy will be most helpful to the community . . . when it is apparent that the one who is preacher in the pulpit and priest before the altar is also pastor to the community."[5]

In this chapter three homileticians will suggest ways to approach preaching from a pastoral perspective. Kathy Black has developed a "healing homiletic" that addresses the particular concerns of those who are disabled; Leonora Tubbs Tisdale understands the preacher's role as a caretaker of "local theology" and a dancer who shares the floor with church tradition, the biblical text, and each member of a congregation; and Christine Smith invites us to consider the preacher as one who weaves together the various and colorful strands of the biblical text and congregational concern.

Kathy Black: A Healing Homiletic

Kathy Black challenges those who preach, "Where is the gospel, the good news for persons with disabilities?"[6] The answer, of course, is that the church has long neglected and in some instances done harm to those in our communities with disabilities. In order to preach to those with disabilities, Black offers four guidelines:

1) *Be cautious when making generalizations.* "In the case of persons with disabilities, each person's situation is so very different that it is difficult to know the transformations possible for individual circumstances."[7]

2) *Be open to our definitions of healing and wholeness.* "The possibility of transformation is present at every moment of our lives."[8] We might consider someone who is deaf and blind as "full of suffering and loneliness." But Black reminds us a blind person can hear nuances of a Mozart symphony and a deaf person can feel the grooves of a sculpture we might ordinarily miss.

3) *God is not to blame for disabilities.* "Devastations, sufferings, frustrations, and disabilities happen in this world. God does not cause them, but God is present in their midst to uphold us and transform us. Resurrection can happen in our lives without God causing the suffering and death in order for the resurrection to occur. God's grace is all-powerful and can turn pain into healing."[9]

4) *We are all interdependent.* "God wills the well-being of each of us at every moment of our lives. At the same time, we are

all interdependent upon one another and upon the natural world. God depends on us to be God's agents of healing in the world as much as we depend on God to undergird us with everlasting love and care."[10]

A Healing Homiletic

Black challenges us therefore to "nurture an interdependent community where we are agents of the daily miraculous transformations God wills for each of our lives."[11] This she calls "a healing homiletic." In her book, she offers five guidelines that define a "healing homiletic" and assist in preaching texts where healing occurs:

1) "In preaching [healing texts] comparisons can be made, as long as sensory language is not used, in relationship to sin. Instead of saying we are *blind, deaf, mute, or paralyzed*, to the will of God, we should say what we mean: 'we do not understand who Jesus is,' 'we ignore God's will for our lives.'"[12]

2) "[Highlight that] most of the people with disabilities described in the texts are ostracized and rejected by their social and religious communities, not because of some sinful act they committed, but simply because of some aspect of who they are—some part of their being."[13]

3) "[Notice that] Jesus breaks the ritual purity code . . . , [ask] what unwritten purity codes are operating in your congregation? What boundaries have our communities of faith established to protect themselves from those considered unclean today?"[14]

4) "Emphasize the actions of the person with the disability in the text. . . . How can we enable people in their search for well-being when our tendency is to judge those who take the initiative—when we feel they should stay on the margins?"[15]

5) "Focus on the response of the crowds. . . . How do we respond to the unfamiliar, the out-of-the-ordinary, those who are unlike us?"[16]

Black's emphasis on healing that occurs regardless of a cure speaks not only to those with physical disabilities, but all who come to church carrying burdens. As she reminds, "the possibility of transformation is present at every moment of our lives."[17]

Leonora Tubbs Tisdale: Preaching as Local Theology and Folk Art

Leonora Tubbs Tisdale believes good preaching arises from a careful and thorough "exegesis" of the congregation. In her opinion, preachers need to become "amateur ethnographers—skilled in observing and in thickly describing the subcultural signs and symbols of the congregations they serve."[18] She recommends we strive to speak in specifics, not generalizations. "[We must] return to the spirit of Jesus whose own proclamation of God's reign was marked by its fittingness for farmers and fisherfolk, for servants and landowners, for Pharisees and tax collectors."[19]

By paying attention to the particular joys and concerns of a community, the preacher is able to piece together what Tisdale calls "local theology . . . theology that not only takes seriously larger church traditions, but that also attends with equal seriousness to the world view, life experiences, and prior traditions of her own very particular congregation."[20] Sermons should be prepared with an awareness of how "people already imagine God and the world" and never for "generic humanity." In order to authentically speak from a place within the community, Tisdale recommends we ask exegetical questions not only of a biblical text but of our congregation as well. Questions such as:

1) Who are identified as heroes in the stories of congregational life? Who are the villains?
2) Where are the silences in the storytelling of the congregation?
3) Is there a common dream that unites the congregation?
4) If you were to plot the story of the congregation, what would it look like?
5) What types of activities or events receive the most attention?[21]

Preaching as Local Theology

After exegeting the congregation and discerning its "local theology," Tisdale suggests we then imagine ourselves as dancers, extending a hand to various partners: "Scripture, congregational context, church doctrine."[22] Our sermon preparation does not begin only with a biblical text but "the process is more accurately described as moving from 'con/text' (a term that can mean either 'context,' or 'with the text,' or both) to sermon."[23] We might ask of the text: "What would my people doubt to be true in this text?" "With what inner feelings, longings, thoughts, and desires of my people does this text connect?"[24] Tisdale does not offer a sermon structure that can best reflect the local theology of a community but maintains that "preaching as folk art allows form itself to emerge out of the unique meeting of text and context."[25]

Ultimately, what is central in Tisdale's model is that the preacher strives "to prepare sermons that are hearer-oriented—sermons in which preacher meets congregants on their ground, rather than requiring congregants to meet preacher on his or her ground."[26]

Christine Smith: Weaving the Sermon

While Tisdale offers the image of the preacher as dancer, Christine Smith appropriates the image of the weaver as a model for pastoral preaching. She writes, "Learning how to weave has affirmed for me the truth that in any craft, be it weaving or preaching, one must balance structure and creativity, principles of design and form with imagination and vision."[27] What Smith weaves through the loom of structure, creativity, imagination, and vision are the stories of our lives and the stories of our congregation. The goal is to articulate the "web of human relatedness" in which all participants share an equal role. A faithful preacher understands that, "The preacher speaks on behalf of the community, never abdicating one's own voice but also never allowing one's own voice to dominate or silence others. . . . The weaving is done by all."[28]

At the core of Smith's homiletical model is an emphasis on relationship and self-disclosure. She writes, "If preaching is fundamentally a relational act, preachers also need to bring the fullness of who they are to the task."[29] While Tisdale invites us to "exegete" the congregation, Smith invites the entire congregation into the pastor's study. Questions she recommends asking during sermon preparation include: "What are we trying to explore, create, or articulate together?" "What can we all see together in these moments of proclamation?" "What do you illumine for me in terms of mystery and faith, what do I illumine for you, and what truths can we bring to light together?"[30]

While helpfully framing the sermon process as "intimate" and deeply rooted in the relationship between pastor and congregation, Smith's model is not without its critics. Carol Noren, for example, cautions that an overemphasis on self-disclosure may not always serve the preacher well. She writes, "The stereotype being reinforced in such self-disclosure is that in relationships, women always want more. They're pushing for greater emotional intimacy than the other party is ready to give."[31] Long agrees and adds that in focusing so intensely on the relationship between pastor and congregation, in Smith's model there is "aching loneliness . . . [for] there is no saving Word from outside."[32]

Long also offers three cautions for preaching from a pastoral perspective.

1) In the concern to address problems in the congregation, the church's mission or strengths can be forgotten.
2) Sometimes there is no answer to a problem an individual or congregation is facing, and all we can do is "point to the future, which belongs to God."
3) Ultimately, we need to ask if as preachers we are to "help people find their stories in the Bible, or make the story of the Bible their story."[33]

Robert Coles tells of a friend who was dying from cancer. When the hospital chaplain came to visit, all he wanted to talk about was his friend's "feelings" or "stress." Coles's friend was frustrated; he wanted to talk about "God and His ways, about Christ's life and death, about Heaven and Hell.[34] Finally, the friend decided to force the issue and the next time the chaplain came for a visit, before the priest could speak, he picked up a Bible from the nightstand and invited him to read from it, any part, it didn't matter.

Pastoral preaching reminds the preacher we minister within a context of a congregation who come to church with specific worries, concerns, and needs. To ignore that fact is to preach as a prophet and, ultimately, outside the community. Black, Tisdale, and Smith invite us to sit in the pews and partner with a congregation in the crafting of a sermon. But as Long and Noren caution, the focus should never be only on our problems, but the grace and love God offers to each of us. When successful, pastoral preaching acknowledges and responds to our deepest needs, and, as Fosdick writes, it engineers an "operation by which a chasm is bridged so that spiritual goods on one side—the 'unsearchable riches of Christ'—are actually transported into personal lives upon the other."[35]

SERMONS

"Opening Our Eyes"

Amy E. Richter   Mark 10:46–52

Today's gospel lesson tells the story of the blind man, Bartimaeus, who is healed by Jesus. The ancients called sight "the Queen of the Senses." What is more lovely than seeing the sunrise, or the deep royal blue of the sky before dawn, the smile on your beloved's face, the deep red leaves of a Japanese maple in the fall? You can imagine your own feast for the eyes, sights that delight or intrigue, sights that you wish to savor. I remember as a child, being on a family vacation, driving along the shore of Lake Superior at sunset, brilliant reds and oranges and the fiery globe of the sun were reflected in the vast stretch of water. I thought, I want to remember this scene forever, and so far I have. Think of the beauty of St. Chrysostom's garden. Or the way the sun lights up the blue in the stained glass windows up there on a Sunday morning.

To be blind would be to miss these blessings. But there are many kinds of blindness. The *New York Times* once reported a story about women who had witnessed the horror of the Killing Fields in Cambodia. Members of their families had been killed while they were forced to watch. These women are now blind, although there is no physical cause of blindness. Such psychological blindness seems a tragic, but understandable, consequence for people who have seen more than they can bear.

Sometimes we suffer a psychological blindness of a lesser kind, not permanent: a *choosing* not to see, a turning of a blind eye when we are confronted by someone, something we would rather not see. A man, dirty and smelling of alcohol, boarded the el in the car where I was sitting. His voice broke the relative quiet of the ride. "This is hard for me to do," he announced thickly, "but I want to sing for you." And he sang, in a drunk and wandering kind of way, a tune with unintelligible words. And then he asked for donations. Everyone looked anywhere but at the man. "I can't blame you for ignoring me," he said. His catching us in the act only made our desire not to notice more urgent. Some people studied the floor like it was a final exam. Some gazed intently at the advertisements above, as if we might miss crucial information such as the key to happiness in life. "I can't blame you for looking away," slurred the man. "I know I'm a terrible sight."

And there is blindness, permanent, physical blindness, like the kind

Bartimaeus suffered in today's gospel lesson. Look with me at blind Bartimaeus.

Perhaps the worst part of going blind was losing his independence. Bartimaeus had enjoyed going where he wanted to go, doing what he wanted, when he wanted. Now, blind, he was dependent on strangers. On passersby. On a good day for business in Jericho. On sunshine and good moods. On holidays. On whatever might turn the hearts of a stranger in this big city to drop a few coins onto his cloak, spread out in front of him, a beggar. The world, which had once been so full of sights, so full of possibilities, so full of places he might one day go and see, had been narrowed to a small space on the pavement, just large enough for the blind man to crouch with his outspread cloak.

He knew what a pitiful sight he must be: crouched low, wrapped in his scratchy cloak, the fabric worn from use and faded by the sun, his watery eyes searching but not seeing. Shameful. Painful to look at. And he *knew* that passersby averted their eyes even though he couldn't see them. He could hear their voices fade as they turned their heads aside, saying, "Sorry," as they passed, looking away. And there were those who stared. He could feel it. People got closer, wanting a look at this pitiful blind man.

They say the eyes are the window to the soul. When people saw his eyes, they saw nothing. Blinking eyes, empty, nothing beyond, nothing beneath.

But Bartimaeus knew there was something there beneath his sightless eyes. Deep in his heart there was a dream, a desire—that he could see again. More than anything, in his heart of hearts, he wanted to see. He held onto his dream, and he would play it over and over to himself. He would imagine himself, with his sight restored, a free man. No longer dependent on anyone. If he could see, he would be free. Free to stand up, put on his cloak, and go. Go. Free. Shake off the dust of Jericho as he left. He could be his own man once again.

One day Bartimaeus sits, fingering the fraying threads of a forming hole in his cloak, his chin lifted, eyes open but unseeing, listening. Listening. A large crowd approaches. Such a crowd is nothing new on this road, yet there is something different, an urgency, excitement. Talk of going to Jerusalem for the Passover celebration. Snippets of people's plans for their journey to the Holy City. Bartimaeus strains to sift out one voice from another, strains to hear what they are saying as they approach him. He hears voices mingled, conversing, pieces of a story or a song. And then, one word. A name, on someone's lips—spoken, then gone—but Bartimaeus hears: Jesus. It is Jesus of Nazareth who passes. He has heard this name before. Overheard as people passed. He has heard the man by this name has the power to heal—to make whole—to make dreams come true—to make Bartimaeus's dream come true, his dream of freedom, a life free from begging, a life of independence, of not having to be dependent on others, a life where he can stand up, wrap his cloak around his shoulders, and go where he wills.

Jesus. He hears the name so distinctly amidst the din of voices in the noisy crowd: Jesus.

He cries out—his voice dry and raspy—"Jesus, Son of David, have mercy on me!"

"Be quiet, beggar!" a voice close to him snaps. "Quiet down." Someone tosses him a coin. "Be quiet."

But the beggar's voice, gaining strength, cries out again, "Son of David, have mercy on me!" And he hears the footsteps of one person stop. And a voice, a man's voice up ahead, says, "Call him here."

More voices close by, "Take heart, beggar. Get up. He is calling you."

It happens so fast. He realizes his chance, his moment, his opportunity. He throws off his cloak, he springs to his feet, he runs toward the voice that called to him, Jesus' voice.

Jesus says to him, "What do you want me to do for you?"

"My teacher," Bartimaeus says, "let me see again."

Jesus replies, "Go. Your faith has made you well."

The first thing Bartimaeus notices is the light, how bright the daylight is as it floods his view, as the heat of the sun on his back is joined with the sunlight flooding his eyes. The din of the crowd fades as he sees shapes and colors that meld into people, lights, and shadows that he recognizes as faces, eyes looking back at him in amazement, not pity, but wonder, and the one face, the face of Jesus, his eyes looking into his eyes, so close, so intent, the face of the healer seeing him.

And then Bartimaeus remembers the word, like a distant dream. Jesus had said it, "Go." Go. Bartimaeus, you are free. To go. Where you will. Go.

And Bartimaeus realizes this is not what he wants from his freedom. He does not wish to leave this man, this one who asked him his heart's desire, this one who didn't presume to know, this one who heard his reply, who listened to his dream, this one who set him free. And he realizes that he no longer wishes to go where *he* wills. He wishes to follow. To use his gift of sight for something, not just for himself. He is freed, to follow.

And Bartimaeus follows Jesus on the way.

Years later, when the disciples told the story of their friend Bartimaeus, they joked about their own blindness, their inability to see the significance of who Jesus was, even when he was standing right there in front of them, plain as day. They laughed because they had missed it so often, and this blind man, Bartimaeus, could see clearly who Jesus was, without even laying eyes on him. With the eyes of his heart, Bartimaeus could see the truth.

The disciples told Bartimaeus's story because Bartimaeus did *not* go. He came with them and followed Jesus on the way. This meant taking the journey first to Jerusalem, where Jesus would die on the cross, a painful, shameful sight, and most disciples averted their eyes. After the resurrection, the first name of their movement, even before they used the name Christian, was the Way. The way is not easy. But we are not alone. Bartimaeus received his sight and freedom and he used it rightly, to follow. To declare his dependence on the Always Dependable One.

They told Bartimaeus's story because Jesus left them with a challenge: Jesus would not always be with them physically, in plain view. They would not always be able to see him. But Jesus promised to remain with them, to be known to them in the breaking of bread, in the hearing of the Word, in the face of a friend or a stranger. He told them to use the eyes of their hearts, because there are many different kinds of blindness.

They told Bartimaeus's story, and we tell the story, because seeing, really seeing, is hard work. We all have our blind spots, and those things we would turn our eyes away from. God needs people whose hearts are trained to see the glory of God at work in the world, whose eyes are trained to look with compassion, whose vision is courageous. Jesus, who made the blind Bartimaeus to see, can heal all our blindness also.

Jesus calls to us: What do you want me to do for you?

Oh, answer him! Raise your voice. He has set us free. Leap up. Throw off the cloak of blindness. Ask God to open your eyes to what God longs to show you. And follow on the way.

Amy E. Richter is the associate rector at the Saint Chrysostom's Church, Chicago, Illinois.

"The Gospel We Don't Want to Hear (or Preach)"

Leonora Tubbs Tisdale   Gen. 45:1–15, Luke 6:27–36

It was a number of months ago when I finally admitted to myself that there was something at the very heart of our Christian gospel that I not only did not want to hear, but that I no longer knew how to preach.

It was January. I had a preaching engagement coming round the bend at a New York City church where one of my former students is serving as associate pastor—a church that follows the Common Lectionary in its preaching. So I turned to see what the texts were for the Seventh Sunday after Epiphany. The first text I read was the Gospel text this evening from Luke. All I needed was the first line to let me know that I didn't want to touch this one with a ten-foot pole. "But I say to you that listen, Love your enemies, do good to those who hate you, bless those who curse you, pray for those who abuse you."

I still remember sitting in my study at home and literally groaning aloud as I read that text because, you see, at the time I had within me considerable anger toward some people who had hurt someone I care about, and the last thing I wanted to hear was a gospel that required me to love my enemies and to forgive those who had done such evil.

It seemed to me at the time a cheap grace—one that required restitution of relationship at the expense of any communal demand for righteousness and justice, forgiveness without any sign of repentance or change of heart on the part of the enemy, love without any admission on the part of evildoers that their deeds had been loveless. Not only did I not want to hear this Gospel; I knew I was in no place in my personal life to preach it convincingly. So, I moved on to the Old Testament, thinking surely there I would find an escape from such gospel-speech.

But there I encountered the Old Testament text we also read this evening: the text where Joseph not only forgives his brothers who sold him into slavery years before—without any sign whatsoever that they are penitent (indeed they seem a lot more fearful than penitent in this text). Joseph also tells them that God meant all this for good, and how glad he is that he was able to come before them to Egypt so that he could provide food for them in their time of famine.

By this time my groaning had turned to moaning, and I began to see that there was no escape here. I even began to think that God—with some wicked notion of divine humor—had sent me these texts so that I would have to live with them and wrestle with them, and clean up my own act in the process.

So, for two days, I tried. I prayed over these texts, I read about them in commentaries, and finally, in desperation, I pulled off my shelf Martin Luther King's book of sermons entitled *Strength to Love* so that I could glean wisdom from someone who knew what it was to have real enemies, and to face real injustice, and to wrestle with these texts in light of a horribly sinful reality. And then I dutifully called my former student to give her my sermon title for the bulletin, based on those lectionary texts.

My student, however, seemed puzzled. "You're not preaching on the texts for Transfiguration Sunday?" she said. And then I realized my mistake. Being at home at the time, and not having my trusty sermon planning calendar at my side, I had looked up the texts for the Seventh Sunday after Epiphany in the Presbyterian Church's *Book of Common Worship*. But in that particular year, the Seventh Sunday after Epiphany was also Transfiguration Sunday. And, it was clear that the worship at this church had been planned with a Transfiguration theme in mind.

So, seeing before me a way of escape from my ordeal, I eagerly took it. "Of course," I said, "I would love to preach on that text where Moses comes down from the mountain after visiting with God and his face shines so much it scares people. Sign me up! And I'll call you shortly with a new sermon title."

For many months, then, this sermon lay unfinished, haunting me. Haunting me because increasingly I realized that I did not know how to complete it, that I honestly do not know how to preach that love of enemies and that radical forgiveness that lies at the heart of the Christian gospel.

I do not know how to preach "love of enemies" and "forgiving as we are forgiven" in a world where women and children are physically beaten and battered in homes, and where the preaching of this gospel in the Christian church has often forced those women prematurely to swallow their own justified rage; has added to the immeasurable burdens they already bear by placing upon them, the victims, the burden of having to "forgive" that abusing spouse, and which, at its worst, has sent those women back to be reconciled with and to "love" the very ones who place their lives in danger.

I do not know what it means to preach "forgiveness" in a country where Billy Graham, viewed by many as the closest person this nation has to a high priest, went on national television in the midst of the latest presidential scandal and pronounced his own forgiveness and absolution of Bill Clinton—before there was any admission of wrongdoing or any sign of repentance on the part of the president. Is forgiveness this easy, this light, this nondemanding?

And I do not know how to preach love of enemies and forgiveness in a Kosovo kind of world. Or in a world where, earlier this year, two former leaders of the Khmer Rouge in Cambodia—a regime that we now know was responsible for the deaths of about one million people several decades ago—surrendered themselves, asking that their nation "let bygones be bygones"—and in which the prime minister of that land offered to receive them with open arms. Is this what the gospel means by forgiveness? That we cheapen the death of one million human beings by saying, "The past is past. Let bygones by bygones. Let's forgive and forget and get on with our lives"?

While our culture and even our church often equate forgiving and forgetting, I don't see that our gospel does. There is too much in these scriptures of ours that speaks of God's own outrage against injustice and the cheapening of human life—whatever form it may take.

Indeed, it is very interesting to me to note that this passage from Luke's Gospel about loving enemies is immediately preceded by the "blessings and woes," Luke's version of the Beatitudes.

Listen to what Jesus says here—just before his teaching about love and forgiveness:

> "Blessed are you who are poor, for yours is the kingdom of God.
> Blessed are you who are hungry now, for you will be filled.
> Blessed are you who weep now, for you will laugh.
> Blessed are you when people hate you, and when they exclude
>   you, revile you, and defame you on account of the Son of
>   Man.
> Rejoice in that day and leap for joy, for surely your reward is
>   great in heaven;
> For that is what their ancestors did to the prophets.
>
> But woe to you who are rich, for you have received your con-
>   solation.
> Woe to you who are full now, for you will be hungry.
> Woe to you who are laughing now, for you will mourn and
>   weep.
> Woe to you when all speak well of you,
>   for that is what their ancestors did to the false prophets."
>   (Luke 6:20–26)

Whatever we say about "loving enemies" and "forgiving others" we cannot say that it means a cheap discounting of the unjust actions of others, a quick dismissal of the persecutions born by those who are victims of injustice, or a facile embrace of the enemy that does not hold the perpetrator of evil accountable to God and others.

Jesus here reminds us that God has a special compassion for those who suffer injustice in this life. They are "blessed" in the realm of God's reign—not because their suffering is glorified, but because God remembers them and will one day vindicate them.

And as for the evildoers, it is quite clear here, as in other places in scripture, that they will be held accountable by God. When the cosmic tables of injustice in this world are overturned by God, those who once sat at them—trafficking in manipulation and control and exploitation and false accusations of God's people—will be in a state of "woe." Their laughing over exploitive victories in this world will be changed to mourning and weeping, as they encounter the God whose anger is always kindled when people do evil instead of good.

Our culture often equates "forgive and forget" as if they are synonymous terms. But the Gospel of our Lord does not. It is in the very context of God's promised remembering—a remembering those who have suffered evil and a remembering those who have perpetrated it—that these difficult words regarding love and forgiveness come. And whatever they mean, they don't mean that we cheapen the horrific remembrances of those who have suffered great evils by asking them to "forget."

We cannot ask a woman who has been scarred for life by her husband's physical or emotional abuse to "forget" it, and get on with her life.

We cannot ask a country that has been lied to time and time again to simply "forget" that reality, and move on with its common life.

And we cannot ask a world that has watched, and is still watching, the slaughter of the innocent by despotic leaders to simply "let bygones be bygones" and move on with its life. To do so is a denial of the gospel, not a true proclamation of it.

Nor does forgiveness, in a biblical understanding, always mean a resumption of former relationships, a *return* to things as they were. In the culture of the church, we have often equated forgiveness with a returning, a patching up and getting on with life as it was, a willingness to go back and commit to the relationship once again.

And surely forgiveness does sometimes mean a "returning." All of us here could tell stories about occasions in our own relationships and in the relationships of others in which miracles of reconciliation have occurred, where relationships that seemed beyond healing have been healed and restored by the grace, mercy, and forgiveness of God and of human beings.

But David Augsburger, a professor of pastoral care at Fuller Theological Seminary, also cautions us against equating forgiving with "returning." In his most recent book, *Helping People Forgive,*

Augsburger writes that forgiveness that is about *returning* can be dangerous and harmful; it can simply be "a restitution of an old order, a backward movement, a regression to the previous situation with the old injustices that motivated the original action or injury."[36] That kind of forgiveness has the potential to enslave the one who has been wronged by forcing that person to yield once again to old ways of living and relating that are defined not by God but by sinfully corrupt human institutions.

Forgiveness according to the gospel, says Augsburger, is more about *turning* than "returning." It is a *revolution,* a progression into a new situation, a transformation that alters the status quo, that challenges the many compromises that create our systems—be they cultural, religious, communal, family, marital, or whatever.[37] "Jesus does not forgive as a means of returning people to the *status quo.* His actions are directed at transforming them, at breaking them out of the limited vision of culture and idol so that they catch a glimpse of the true God beyond . . . the culture's moral system."[38]

One of the dangers I see in the church today is that we too facilely and easily make forgiveness a matter of "returning" rather than of "turning," and by so doing we blur too quickly the systemic issues that are bound up with the personal ones. We ask people personally to forgive and return to a relationship, and in so doing send them back into systems where there is a radical inequality of corrupted power, and where there is no possibility—until that system of injustice changes—that they will be dealt with fairly and equitably, no matter the professions of repentance on the part of an individual.

James Cone, systematic theologian at Union Theological Seminary in New York and author of numerous books on Black liberation theology, was recently on the Princeton Seminary campus inaugurating our Martin Luther King Jr. lectureship. Cone's address entitled "Martin and Malcolm on Non-Violence and Violence"[39] was stirring and deeply challenging in a context where, as Cone himself laughingly predicted, we would have more trouble swallowing Malcolm X than Martin King. But Cone insisted throughout his lecture that both leaders had been critical for the liberation of his people, and he refused to let us too easily dismiss Malcolm in order to embrace Martin.

During the question-and-answer period Cone described his own commitment to living within the tension posed by the two most succinctly when he said this: "Martin [King] wouldn't let me let go of the fact that I'm a Christian. But Malcolm never let me forget that I am also Black. For me the goal of all I'm about is the oneness of all humanity. We were made to live in relationship with one another. But for me that also means that I cannot live in a false relationship with those who consistently demean and devalue my worth as a child of God. I cannot re-enter a relationship with someone who refuses to treat me as a person of worth, an equal. To do so is to return again to slavery."[40]

It has been interesting to me this time around, reading the story of Joseph's forgiveness and embrace of his brothers, to think about that story not only interpersonally (as I have always done), but also systemically (as I have never before done). When viewed through a purely personal lens, this saga becomes one more incentive for those who have been abused through sick family systems to forgive and to enter back into relationship with one's relatives, no matter what heinous crimes they have committed.

But if viewed systemically, this story takes on a whole new meaning. Note that in the intervening time between the selling of Joseph by his brothers into slavery and their encounter in this text, the balance of power in this relationship has also radically changed. Joseph, once the weaker brother, is now the strongest brother: a ruler in Pharaoh's court with the literal ability to make life-and-death decisions regarding the lives of those brothers who once abused him.

By forgiving his brothers in this new social context, Joseph in no way signals a *returning* to the old, unjust, and inhumane ways of living within his family. Rather, I see in Joseph's forgiveness a model of the *turning* of which Augsburger speaks.

Instead of using the power now entrusted to him for evil, Joseph uses it for good. Through his act of personal forgiveness Joseph pronounces an end to the status quo order of governance of the world (rule by manipulation, control, and vengeance), and the beginning of a new reign in which the mercy and compassion of God will be manifest in the attitude of the ruler toward the ruled.

Perhaps we in the church have been preaching the Joseph story to the wrong people. Rather than preaching Joseph to victims—telling them they should repent and forgive those who abuse them, we should be preaching Joseph to the powerful—encouraging them to embrace God's new way of mercy and compassion rather than the world's way of vindictiveness and retribution. Joseph is no model for enslaving servitude. Rather, Joseph models servant leadership, the kind we ultimately see revealed in the one from Nazareth whose own words about forgiveness continue to haunt us.

If Christian forgiveness, then, is not about a facile "returning" that requires no change in the status quo, and if forgiveness is not about a false "forgetting" that refuses to name evil for what it is, what is it? What is Christian forgiveness?

Certainly we glimpse something of its radical core in the words of Jesus as they come to us this evening in Luke 6, and in the life and death of the one who spoke those words. "But I say to you that listen, love your enemies, do good to those who hate you, bless those who curse you, pray for those who abuse you. . . . Be merciful, just as your Father is merciful."

Christian forgiveness, whatever we say about it, has its taproots in God's own radical love for us: a love that is persistently, determinedly, unwaveringly merciful, even toward those totally undeserving of that mercy.

Anne Lamott currently has a book on the bestseller list called *Traveling Mercies*, a book in which she recounts her own life lived through the lens of her Christian faith. She begins her section on "Forgiveness" with these words:

> I went around saying for a long time that I am not one of those Christians who is heavily into forgiveness—that I am one of the other kind. But even though it was funny, and actually true, it started to be too painful to stay this way. They say we are not punished for the sin but by the sin, and I began to feel punished by my unwillingness to forgive. By the time I decided to become one of the ones who *is* heavily into forgiveness, it was like trying to become a marathon runner in middle age; everything inside me either recoiled, as from a hot flame, or laughed a little too hysterically.[41]

Lamott goes on to tell a tale about an ordinary, everyday enemy—the parent of one of her children's friends whom she calls "Enemy Light"—and of her own long, slow movement in their testy relationship from anger and a desire for revenge against this woman—whom she felt consistently demeaned her because she wasn't the kind of mother or author this woman thought she should be—to an acknowledgment of their common humanity, and an admission to herself that some of her evil thoughts toward this woman had actually been projections of her own shortcomings.

It was while sitting in this woman's dining room, sharing tea with her while their boys played together, that Lamott says the veil finally lifted, and she finally released and let go much of the anger, resentment, and desire for retaliation she had been holding inside. She describes it this way:

> I felt so happy there in her living room that I got drunk on her tea. I read once in some magazine that in Czechoslovakia, they say an echo in the woods always returns your own call, and so I started speaking sweetly to everyone—to the mother, to the

boys. And my sweet voice started getting all over me, like sunlight, like the smell of the Danish baking in her oven, two of which [my former enemy] put on a paper plate and covered with tin foil for me and Sam [my son] to take home.[42]

Whatever forgiveness means from a Christian point of view, surely it means that over time we Christians have to come to terms with the rage within us—sorting out that rage that is "holy" and of God (the rage that remembers evil) from the rage that is "unholy" and motivated by revenge and retribution—and to let some of that unholy rage go so that there is space, once more, for love.

In an article he wrote for *The Christian Century* in the aftermath of the surrender of the two top officials of the Khmer Rouge regime, Miroslav Wolf, a professor of theology at Yale Divinity School, said that the most astonishing part of that story never made it into the headlines.

"What was truly extraordinary about the surrender and its aftermath was the reaction of some victims. 'When I see them, it is difficult to forgive—very difficult,' said one person who had lost most of his family during the Khmer Rouge years. 'It is just like waking me up when I see them. But we have to forgive and move on.'

"Have to forgive?" asks Wolf incredulously. And then he goes on to posit why many of the victims chose forgiveness over its alternative.

> For some, the wells from which the tears flow have simply dried up, and the fuel which feeds the fires of anger has burned up; after years of mourning and rage, they are tired and want rest. Others realize that they themselves cannot be healed until they have given up resentment and moved on—with or without justice done. Still others believe that their moral dignity will not be restored until they have come to love their enemies; they want to forgive, even to let the misdeeds fall into oblivion, because they refuse to let those who have maimed their bodies mar their souls.[43]

Surely forgiveness, in the first instance, means a release, a letting go of the bitterness within so that we refuse to let those who have maimed our bodies or our spirit or our psyches also maim our souls. The gospel of Christ never lets us off the hook in that regard. It always draws us, urges us toward a new way of being—not solely for the sake of our enemies, but perhaps, primarily, for our own sake. If we will be truly free in Christ, we need to release that bitterness within that keeps us from experiencing the fullness of God's own love for us.

And for some that sorting through and releasing may take a long, long time. We in the church need to learn patience in this regard.

But of course this Gospel text calls for more than a release and letting go of the unholy rage within us. Jesus also calls on us to be proactive: to love our enemies, to do good to those who hate us, to bless those who curse us, and to pray for those who abuse us. We are called to be merciful, even as God is merciful.

And that, of course, is where the real rub of this text comes. What does love look like, when it also goes hand in hand with a remembering of evil, a holding of evildoers accountable, and a refusal to discount evil or sweep it under the rug? What does love look like in a situation in which a "return" to a relationship of equality and respect with the other is simply impossible?

I do not yet know what it looks like for me, personally; I'm still struggling with it. In a very real sense, this sermon is still unfinished for me. And I don't pretend to know what it looks like for you. But I share with you, in closing, three possibilities that have passed my way in recent months as I have wrestled with these matters.

The first possibility was posed for me in a sermon preached this past Valentine's Day by a pastor I know.[44] Wrestling with the whole tough issue of what love looks like when reconciliation of the relationship is not possible, this pastor revisited that scene between Jacob and his uncle Laban at Mizpah where those immortal words, "May the Lord watch between me and thee, while we are absent one from the other," are spoken.

The pastor readily acknowledged that these words are spoken between two people who have little love for one another, and even less trust. By this juncture in the story Laban had tricked Jacob into working for him fourteen long years to marry the daughter originally promised after seven years of work. And Jacob is now getting his revenge by fleeing Laban's house—taking with him both of Laban's beloved daughters, and all possibilities for grandchildren. At Mizpah the two meet, pile up stones, and make a covenant before God. And the covenant is certainly in part a plea to God on behalf of each man to keep the other straight.

But this pastor also noted that even at their point of greatest enmity, these two parted company not with curses, but with a prayer that God would go with them both. While forgiveness and reconciliation were impossible for Jacob and Laban, each sent the other off in the hands of a God who not only judges and remembers evil, but who alone is just. That which they couldn't sort out themselves, they left to God to sort.

I suspect that, in some cases in our own lives, love that does not forsake justice will require us to "shake the dust off our feet" and to move on from relationships where a "turning" from evil and toward good does not seem possible, while still praying for the other and lifting the other up before God as we go.

David Augsburger draws a helpful differentiation between unilateral forgiveness (in which we come to that point personally in which we are able, by the power of the Spirit, to release some of our unholy rage and to see the other once more as a child of God) and mutual forgiveness (in which a relationship with the other is restored and reconstructed). Augsburger says that while the former, grounded in unconditional love, is always required of the Christian, the latter is not. "There may be no demands for seeing the other as worthful and precious," he writes, "but many demands for trusting, risking, and joining in relationship—no demands for loving; many demands for living." Otherwise the grace offered is cheap indeed.[45]

The second and more public model for what forgiveness looks like in a broken world comes to us from the Truth and Reconciliation Commissions in South Africa. As I'm sure you know, these commissions were formed by the South African government to deal with the heinous crimes committed during the rule of apartheid in South Africa, and have been supported by many Christian leaders, including Anglican Bishop Desmond Tutu. In accord with the gospel's radical commands, the commissions hold out the promise of forgiveness, of amnesty for some who come before them. But the grace is not cheap. In order to be forgiven, the perpetrators of crimes must return to the locales where their crimes were committed and, in the presence of the family members and friends of their victims, tell the whole truth about what they have done. They are also required to give satisfactory evidence of a genuine turning of heart and life. A tribunal of highly trained and respected commissioners, in each instance, determines whether the truth has been told, and whether amnesty is warranted.

While I know these commissions have had their detractors, I do believe they are onto something rather profound theologically. Love at its heart requires not only a forgiving, but a remembering—an honest naming of the evil that offends God. Repentance at its heart requires not only confession, but a "turning" of life that signals a new relationship is now possible.

Finally, I return full circle at this sermon's end to one of those places where my quest for understanding forgiveness originally began—to the writings of Martin Luther King himself. I confess that when I went to that volume of King's sermons two years ago, I did so hoping that King would let me off of the love hook. Surely this man, who knew what it was like to have real enemies and real anger over real evils would qualify this radical love of Jesus in some way. But King never did.

Rather I found in King one whose radical strength of love also went hand in hand with a radical, nonviolent resistance of the evil he abhorred, and who, like his Lord, died witnessing to both.

"But I say to you, love your enemies, do good to those who hate you, bless those who curse you, pray for those who abuse you. . . . Be merciful just as your Father is merciful."

May our merciful God give to each of us strength so to love, and wisdom so to live. Amen.

Leonora Tubbs Tisdale is the Elizabeth M. Engle Associate Professor of Preaching and Worship at Princeton Theological Seminary. She has also served as pastor of four churches in central Virginia.

Chapter 8

Biblical Preaching

Preaching is biblical whenever the preacher allows a biblical text to serve as the major means of shaping the content and purpose of the sermon.

William Willimon[1]

Introduction

Most homileticians believe a biblical sermon is one firmly grounded in the bedrock of scripture. Leander Keck, for example, claims preaching is biblical "when it imparts a Bible-shaped word in a Bible-like way."[2] David Bartlett adds that "Right preaching is the interpretation of Scripture . . . but unless it is an interpretation of the text or texts that the congregation has just heard or read aloud, it is not preaching."[3] While the content is understood by most as arising from scripture, the style of biblical preaching style has often varied. In this chapter we will look at two styles perhaps most unfamiliar: preaching an Old Testament text and an expository sermon.

Preaching the Old Testament

Preaching an Old Testament text is for many similar to an Outward Bound course; we wave goodbye to the well-worn trails of the Gospels and venture off into rugged and unfamiliar terrain. We know a guide is essential, but our shelves are full of commentaries on the gospel of Luke, not Zephaniah. One of the main concerns pastors have preaching an Old Testament text is if we should focus only on an Old Testament passage, or balance it with a New Testament pericope? Donald Gowan observes, "The average preacher

I encounter is still not quite sure how (or whether) the Old Testament can be used as a text for a Christian sermon."[4]

Many have attempted to guide the preacher through the homiletical landscape of the Old Testament. Elizabeth Achtemeier, for example, has suggested when preaching an Old Testament text we do pair it with a New Testament passage. "To hear the message of the Old Testament rightly," she argues, "as members of God's covenant people, we must hear the Old Testament in Christ. The pairing of Old and New Testament texts acknowledges that fact. . . . Only by pairing the texts can we hear the whole story."[5]

While Achtemeier's model has guided many preachers since the 1970s, some have wondered if there is another approach. Ronald Allen and John Holbert, for example, suggest that when we pair an Old Testament text with a New Testament text, and interpret the Old Testament through Jesus, we rob "ancient Israel of its integrity. From this perspective, Israel did not enjoy the full blessing of God but existed a murky and unfulfilled preview of Jesus and the church."[6] Allen and Holbert recommend the "preacher first explore the possibility of letting a passage from the Hebrew Bible speak on its own. When the preacher brings the Second Testament or Christ or Christian doctrine or practice into the sermon, let it be for specific and significant reasons."[7]

If we are uncertain as to which guide to follow—Achtemeier or Allen and Tolbert—Fred Craddock suggests we turn to the writers of the New Testament. He notes, "It is of some help and no small comfort to realize that New Testament writers experienced the same struggle over continuity and discontinuity between Old and New."[8] With these writers, notes Craddock, we discover various understandings of how the Old and New Testaments relate to one another. For example, some writers underscore that Jesus was the fulfillment of the law, and others advocate that he came to abolish it. To faithfully preach the Old Testament, Craddock recommends that "each preacher has to think through the question and arrive at a view congenial with the church's position on the Old Testament and one's own theology."[9] To assist in that process of discernment, Craddock offers examples of how various gospels and letters interpret the Old Testament.

> —Matthew's Christ came to fulfill the law and the prophets.
> —The writer of Hebrews developed his argument *a fortiori,* from the lesser to the great. In times past, God was revealed in different manners and degrees, but in these last days he is revealed in a Son.

—Paul placed himself in direct continuity with Abraham and Sarah, but in sharp discontinuity with those who placed Moses and the Law at the center of Judaism.

—Luke set Christ and the church within the story begun with Adam, continued through Israel, and proclaimed finally by the apostles and the Christian evangelists.[10]

Craddock concludes that "somewhere among these and other positions not here described the preacher will stand to read and to preach from the Old Testament texts."[11]

Walter Brueggemann: Preaching Among Exiles

As an example of Allen and Tolbert's model of letting an Old Testament passage stand on its own, Walter Brueggemann directs our homiletical attention towards the "exilic" texts of the Old Testament and invites us to forge connections between life today and the exile of the Israelites. He writes, "I propose that in our preaching and more general practice of ministry we ponder the interface of our *circumstance of exile* and the *scriptural resources* that grew from and address the faith crisis of exile."[12]

In other words, if we come to understand, as Brueggemann suggests, that the church exists today in a state of exile—church growth stagnant, society indifferent to Christian perspectives and interests—then preaching Old Testament "exilic" texts emerges as an essential part of our homiletical canon. Brueggemann offers "six interfaces" between our time and the original exilic period.[13]

1) *"Exiles must grieve their loss and express their resentful sadness about what was and now is not and will never be again."* Just as the Israelites faced displacement, we face a similar passing of our "glory days" with economic and emotional displacement prevalent amongst our families. For scriptural resources, Brueggemann points us towards the book of Lamentations.

2) *"Exile is an act of being orphaned, and many folk sense themselves in that status. There is no sure home, no old family place, no recognizable family food."* Passages that resonate with being isolated include Lamentations and parts of Isaiah. These texts remind us our family includes not only blood relatives, but the whole household of faith.

3) *"The most obvious reality and greatest threat to exiles is the power of despair."* Brueggemann notes the Israelites were in

despair after they lost their faith in God's faithfulness and God's power to save them. With many in our congregations facing despair in their personal, vocational, and spiritual lives, scriptural texts that are helpful include Isaiah 40—55.

4) *"Exile is an experience of profaned absence."* This type of absence, suggests Brueggemann, was particularly felt during the fall of Jerusalem. Suddenly, God was seemingly absent from the Israelites' liturgical and everyday lives. To preach this "interface," Brueggemann points the preacher towards Ezekiel 9—10.

5) *"Exile is an experience of moral incongruity."* As we gaze upon a world of natural disasters and senseless violence, Brueggemann wonders if it is fair to ask if someone else is at fault, *besides ourselves.* "In the Old Testament," remarks Brueggemann, "the thought that God is implicated in a morally incoherent world surfaces in the book of Job."

6) *"The danger in exile is to become so preoccupied with self that one cannot get outside one's self to rethink, reimagine, and redescribe larger reality."* In the midst of an exile from ourselves, society, or even from God, scriptural resources that address the peril of becoming self-absorbed include Esther and Daniel.

With these scriptural resources in hand, Brueggemann suggests that we then preach "exilic" texts with the understanding we are witnesses testifying to God's faithfulness. Our charge is to articulate "the narration and nurture of a counter identity, the enactment of the power of hope in a season of despair, and the assertion of a deep, definitional freedom from the pathologies, coercions, and seductions that govern our society."[14]

Expository Preaching

James Earl Massey notes that, "Would-be expositors will find themselves in a noble and select tradition of workers . . . Origin . . . Donald Grey Barnhouse . . . George Buttrick . . . James Stewart."[15] Expository preaching even makes a case for being one of our oldest styles of preaching. Ronald Allen writes that, "This approach to preaching first appeared in full dress in the community that wrote the Dead Sea Scrolls at Qumran. Several of the scrolls are in this form. Early in the Common Era many of the rabbis employed it."[16] Summing up the tone and confidence of many expository preachers, John Stott declares that, "All true Christian preaching is expository preaching."[17]

But many mainline pastors have dismissed such preaching as bible study dressed in homiletical vestments; a style best left to radio preachers. But in its defense, Ronald Allen notes that what separates an "expository" from a "narrative" or "topical" sermon is merely that it unwaveringly *begins and remains* with the Biblical text. Allen writes that, "The expository sermon originates in the exposition of a biblical text or theme. The text is a window through which to look at the gospel in relationship to the congregation."[18]

In other words, an expository sermon intentionally moves from text to human concern, and not the other way around. William Willimon admits in his recent book, *The Intrusive God*, that his orientation to what might be considered "expository" has changed. He writes, "Too much of my preaching begins at what I judge to be 'where people are.' I begin with their experience, their 'felt need,' then, in twenty minutes, I attempt to move them to the gospel. This renders the gospel into nothing more than a helpful resource to get us what we wanted before we met the gospel."[19]

Expository preaching begins with scripture and holds fast to the text throughout the sermon. The choice an expository preacher makes is what portion of the text to expound: verse-by-verse or by scriptural passage.

John MacArthur: Verse-by-Verse

John MacArthur, a staunch supporter of preaching verse-by-verse, believes such preaching enables a congregation to understand scripture within its particular context. He compares preaching verse-by-verse with how we read a personal letter:

> If I received five letters in the mail one day, it would make no sense to read a sentence or two out of one, skip two, read a few sentences out of another, and go to the next one and read a few out of that, and on and on. If I really want to comprehend the letter—what is going on, the tone, the spirit, the attitude, and the purpose—I must start from the beginning and go to the end of each one. If that is true of personal correspondence, then how much more is it so of divine revelation.[20]

A benefit of developing this scriptural context for a congregation is that it promotes "biblical literacy."[21] Robert Thomas, a homiletical colleague of MacArthur, remarks that, "The final test of the effectiveness of Bible exposition is how well individuals who hear the sermon can go home and read the passage with greater comprehension of its exact meaning than they could before they hear the message."[22] To craft such a sermon, MacArthur makes the following suggestions:

1) *The sermon must have unity.* One of first proponents of expository preaching, John Broadus, declared the "prime requisite" of an expository sermon was "unity."[23] MacArthur understands this unity as reflected in establishment of a sermon's theme, a theme that accomplishes two things: First, "It is crystal clear so that your people know exactly what you are saying." Second, it prevents the sermon from "randomly meandering through a passage."[24]

2) *An expository sermon uses few illustrations.* MacArthur suggests we avoid illustrations. He writes, "Stories have emotional impact, but they are lightweight compared with Scripture. . . . I would rather find a concise analogy or an Old Testament illustration and keep the sermon moving."[25]

3) *Take your time.* "I am convinced," writes MacArthur, "that biblical exposition requires at least forty minutes. . . . It takes fifteen to twenty minutes to give the setting, ten to fifteen minutes to draw out the principles, five to ten minutes to cross-reference them, and give five to ten minutes for a conclusion."[26]

4) *Preach for a decision.* "The goal of preaching is to compel people to make a decision. I want people who listen to me to understand exactly what God's Word demands of them when I am through. Then they must say either, 'Yes, I will do what God says,' or 'No, I won't do what God says.'"[27]

Haddon Robinson: Expository Preaching by Scriptural Unit

Haddon Robinson agrees that an expositor should always stick close to the text. He writes, "The expositor lays down a biblical principle in either his introduction or the first major point, and in the remainder of his message he explores the implications of the principle."[28] But unlike MacArthur, Robinson is willing to open the curtains of his study and have a look around. He remarks that the sermon emerges from "ideas drawn from the Scriptures and related to life." "To preach effectively," writes Robinson, "an expositor must be involved in three different worlds . . . knowledge about the Bible . . . currents swirling across his own times . . . his own particular world."[29]

Robinson also does not recommend only preaching verse-by-verse. He writes that, "A diligent expositor will examine the paragraph breakdowns in both the original texts and the English translations, select the divisions of the material that seem to be the most helpful, and use these as the basis of his exposition."[30] After that selection, we then ask this passage three questions: "What does this mean?" "Is it true?" "What difference does it make?" The aim is to discern the "one emphasis in a text or passage," an emphasis that will enable the expositor to communicate a "biblical concept."[31]

The result that Robinson strives for in a sermon is that the congregation leave inspired to read the passage again: "In the pulpit [the preacher] presents enough of his study to the congregation so that a listener may check the interpretation for himself."[32] To accomplish this Robinson does not ignore the potential of illustrations to "explain, validate, or apply ideas by relating them to tangible experiences."[33] He also asks the congregation to make a decision and writes that, "application gives expository preaching purpose."[34]

Both MacArthur and Robinson preach a biblical style that is unfamiliar to many mainline pastors. But nonetheless, MacArthur makes a strong case for the ability of verse-by-verse preaching to establish the scriptural context of a passage. And Robinson reminds us that a preacher must carefully choose a scriptural passage and then mine that passage for one "biblical concept." Both remind us that, above all, we preach God's word and not our own.

SERMONS

"God Save the Queen!"

Carol Antablin Miles   Esther 1, Matthew 5:3–12

They called it the party of the century. A power dinner to end all power dinners. Everybody who was anybody was invited. Local officials, cabinet members, political patrons. Foreign dignitaries, nobles and governors from all the provinces, from India to Ethiopia. And all sorts of military personnel, from top brass to enlisted men. All had descended on King Ahasuerus's winter palace for what must have been the biggest, most extravagant royal ball ever. It lasted 180 days. That means they partied for six months. And at the end of that time, they threw open the doors of the courtyard and invited in all who were left in the city, great and small, for an additional seven days of feasting and festivities.

Now King Ahasuerus spared no expense when it came to entertaining his guests. Beautiful linens adorned the walls, and couches of silver and gold were brought in to provide extra seating. Drinks were served in golden goblets, no two alike, and the royal wine was flowing, lavished according to the bounty of the king. This must have been the first-ever-recorded "open bar" affair. "Drinking was by flagons," the text says, "without restraint; for the king had given orders to all the officials of his palace to do as each guest desired." At the end of these final seven days it was no wonder that King Ahasuerus was feeling "merry with wine."

But then, all of a sudden, he noticed that something was missing. There were no women at this party. What was a party at the royal palace without beautiful women? Bring on the dancing girls! Wait, he changed his mind. How about just one dancing girl? The most beautiful in all the kingdom. Where were his eunuchs? Have them send for Queen Vashti. Tell her to come. And tell her to wear that slinky black dress. No, no, make it the red one. And tell her not to forget the crown, and the royal jewels. King Ahasuerus wanted everyone to see how incredible she was, and he wanted everyone to know that *she* was *his*.

Well, the message was relayed to Queen Vashti. She was hosting her own dinner party inside the palace for all the women. They were just finishing coffee in the parlor when word came that her presence was requested in the main ballroom. You can imagine her reaction. It was centuries before Tailhook, but Queen Vashti knew that it was not in her best interests to enter a room full of drunken sailors. Even at her husband's behest. So she refused. "No," she said. "Tell my husband I'm not coming."

Needless to say, the royal watchers were all aghast, and King Ahasuerus was furious. It wasn't every day that his commands went unheeded. He was, after all, the most powerful man in the most powerful kingdom in all the world. He quickly gathered his advisors in the war room and asked to be briefed on protocol and precedents. "What, according to the law, is to be done to Queen Vashti because she has not performed according to my command?"

Then one of the king's advisors spoke up. "We can all appreciate the embarrassing predicament your wife has placed you in, your majesty. But you have to understand, this situation cannot be treated as a simple domestic squabble. Queen Vashti's disobedience is a far more serious matter. Not only has she wronged you, she has wronged every man in this kingdom. As soon as our wives hear of it, we will have a revolution on our hands. They will start treating us with contempt, saying, 'Queen Vashti never did what King Ahasuerus told her to do.' When word of this gets out, we will lose control of our wives forever!

"No, if it pleases the king, let us issue a royal decree saying that Queen Vashti has been banished from your sight because of her defiance. And you can give her crown to someone else, someone who is actually worthy of it, your majesty."

All the king's men agreed that this was the message that had to be sent. So Ahasuerus did just as his advisor suggested, and a letter was dispatched to each province declaring that, by order of the king, "Every man shall be master in his own house."

Now, when you're asked to be a guest preacher, especially in a church that you hope will ask you back, it's usually best to preach on something fairly safe. The parable of the prodigal son, the twenty-third psalm, or maybe just the lectionary text for the day. And you would think that I, as a professor of homiletics, would know better than to come here and choose to preach on the story of Queen Vashti. Any Christian minister worth his or her salt knows that we're supposed to be preachers of the gospel, and it's kind of hard to find the gospel in this text.

Oh, I suppose there are some ministers in some segments of the church who actually think they've found it, and it's pretty straightforward. What they hear in this text is a thinly veiled warning to all women: No good can come from failing to obey your husband. Just look at Queen Vashti. Her unwillingness to submit led to the unraveling of her marriage. If we care about having Christian families, we would be wise to remember, "Every man is master of his own house."

But that cannot be the meaning of this text. That is not the word of the Lord (thanks be to God!). Anyone who hears in this story a biblical mandate for "every man master of his house" would have to have missed a very important detail in the telling. These words are not placed on the lips of God, or even one of the prophets of God. They're placed on the lips of a foreign king who was either drunk or royally hung over at the time. What is issued by King Ahasuerus is not a divine decree, but a human decree. And a very human one at that.

I suppose that's what's led some other ministers in some other segments of the church to believe that this story, consequently, has nothing to say to us. They would want to write it off as one of those embarrassing, barbaric Old Testament texts that has no bearing on our lives, and certainly bears no resemblance to the gospel.

But I'm not sure about that. I'm not sure I'm ready to banish this story to the biblical island of misfit texts. Maybe it does relate to the gospel in some way. Maybe there is a word of God for us in the story of Queen Vashti after all. But to understand her story, first we have to understand the story of King Ahasuerus.

It's important to note that when we read Old Testament narratives we're hardly ever privy to people's motivations. So it's significant that at the outset of this text we're told that King Ahasuerus did not throw this big party simply for the enjoyment of his guests. Instead, the text says, all those hundreds of people were invited to be present while he "displayed the great wealth of his kingdom and the splendor and pomp of his majesty." In other words, King Ahasuerus wanted an audience. He wanted an opportunity to show off all his stuff so everyone would know how rich and powerful he was.

We're told in similar language essentially the same thing when he called on Queen Vashti to make an appearance at the banquet wearing the royal crown. He did it, the text says, "in order to show the peoples and the officials her beauty; for she was fair to behold." The implication, of course, is that King Ahasuerus considered her to be just another one of his possessions to be displayed. One more object of beauty adorning his palace like the curtains and the furniture and the table linens.

Now, there is certainly nothing wrong with the fact that she was beautiful, or that he appreciated her beauty. The problem with King Ahasuerus was that he began to value his wife less for who she was and more for her ability to reflect well on him. He began to see her as merely an extension of himself. And in so doing, she became something less than fully human in his eyes.

It would be tempting to distance ourselves from the story at this point, letting it be the problem of some rich old Persian king and his trophy wife. But I wonder if this dynamic is actually much more familiar to us.

We see it most clearly, of course, in couples, but the instinct to value the people in our lives, especially the people closest to us, not for who they are, but for what they can do or be for us, seeps into all kinds of relationships.

I used to teach the senior-high Sunday school class at our church. And one week we were talking about parents who push their children to succeed. We watched a videotape of an interview with this young, good-looking kid who was the captain and quarterback of his high school football team, and his dad. "In our house," the dad was saying, "you can expect us to be involved in just about every moment of Christopher's life. We make sure he eats the right food, we help him think up slogans to put on the team lockers. After the game, no matter what time it is, he and I review the game tape and I point out things that Christopher did well, and help him with things he could improve on. I think I do it to help him know how much I value him as my son."

When I stopped the tape at this point, one of the students wisely observed, "This guy's dad needs to get a life!" I chuckled when she said it, but I also wondered how easily I could be seduced into letting my kids' achievements determine how good I feel about myself. There's a fine line, isn't there, between helping our children become well-rounded or reach their own potential, and living out some aspect of our own agenda through their lives. Whether it's our desire that they play a certain instrument or a certain sport, attend our alma mater or take over the family business, it's easy to forget that our children are not merely an extension of ourselves. They are their own people, with their own dreams and desires, and it is their uniqueness that renders them irreplaceably valuable, apart from anything they can be or do for us.

We face the same temptation in the workplace. I think this is especially true in the towns that we're from, where the pressure to succeed is enormous. It is easy to start thinking of the people who work with us or for us simply in terms of how they can make us look good.

It's a subtle thing. I don't think any of us sets out to treat others in this way. But like Ahasuerus, we are so desperately concerned with appearances, it distorts our vision. And before we know it, we start seeing the people in our lives, even the people we care the most about, as a means to our own ends.

But we can easily end up on the receiving end of this as well. I speak with people all the time, primarily women but not always, who for a whole variety of reasons allow themselves to be treated as less than fully human. Oftentimes it's fear: the fear of violence, of losing a job, or losing a relationship. A woman friend admitted to me recently, with great sadness in her voice, that at this point in her life, a bad relationship was better than no relationship.

Now I know this is nothing new. This is the way the world works, and it's been that way since the days of King Ahasuerus. There are people who use others, and there are people who are used by others. But every now and then, somebody says "no."

Queen Vashti was one of them. She simply refused to be objectified. She refused to be treated as anything less than what she knew herself to be, a queen. And though she lived a few hundred years before Christ came and announced that the kingdom of God is at hand, we catch a glimpse in her life of what that kingdom is all about. And every time you or I resist the temptation to diminish others for our own gain, or refuse to allow ourselves to be diminished, we are staking a claim for God's kingdom come, right here and now.

But saying "no" is not easy. It takes courage. And it often comes with a price. The story of Queen Vashti does not have a happy ending. We don't know exactly what happened to her after the party that night, but we do know that she paid dearly for what she had done. Her refusal cost her everything that mattered in her world. It cost her the throne. But when we see her story through the lens of the gospel, one thing becomes clear: King Ahasuerus could take her crown, but he could not take her majesty.[35]

Carol Miles is associate professor of preaching at Austin Theological Seminary in Austin, Texas.

"Surprises at the Judgment"

Haddon Robinson   Matthew 25:31–46

It's been seven years since I have been part of a graduation here at Denver Seminary, and yet it's all kind of familiar, this graduation. The folks walking down the aisle wearing these kind of silly gowns, faculty brilliant in their plumage, folks eager to get rid of the speaker so they can get onto the serious business of granting degrees. It's all kind of the same.

I notice they still call it a commencement service. That always struck me as strange. Seems to me that for a number of the graduates it's a concluding service. Some of them have been making a career out of theological education. They've taken the courses, read the books, done the assignments, taken the exams, jumped through all the hoops. And now they can be called master of arts or master of divinity or doctor of ministries.

You'd think you would call it a completion rather than a commencement. But they're both true. They've completed it, but now they will go out to use it. A new phase of life is beginning.

It strikes me that what we do here in a commencement service prefigures a time in the future when a phase of history will be completed and another phase of existence will begin, a time when the judges will not be a faculty, a time of judgment in the future. Matthew 25:31–46 is a passage that looks forward to that day in which men and women will be judged. Let me tell you the history of this passage. Not the history you would get in a theological seminary. I mean my own personal history.

The first time I remember hearing this passage I was about twelve. I grew up in the ghetto of New York, and my cousin and I were on a spiritual search: We were looking for a church that had a basketball team. We found one at the Broadway Presbyterian Church, but we also discovered that every silver lining had a cloud, because to play on that team you had to go to Sunday school.

And that's where I fell under the influence of Miss Larch. Miss Larch had a great interest in the events of the last time. It seemed to me she had a particular interest in the judgments. That was probably because of the boys in her class. I remember she talked to us about the judgment of the sheep and the goats. That was back during my literalistic phase of interpretation, and when she talked about the judgment of the sheep and goats I thought she was talking about real sheep, real goats.

The whole thing sounded more like a county fair or a 4-H club, though in those days I wasn't quite sure what a county fair was. I thought it was a little demeaning for Jesus to be judging sheep and goats. But she also told me that God counted all the hairs on our head, and I figured if he's into that trivia, sheep and goats made some sense.

The next time we came back to this passage I was probably fifteen. By that time I had figured out that the passage wasn't really referring to animals. It was referring to people, and the Christians, the good guys, would be called sheep, and the non-Christians would be called goats. I had no idea why Christians would be called sheep. Fifty years later I still don't have much of an idea of why that would be.

A couple of years ago I was out in western Washington talking to man who raises sheep. We're talking fifty thousand of them at a time. I said, "You're into sheep. If you could think of one word that describes sheep, what would it be?" He shot back, "Stupid. They've got to be the stupidest animals you ever work with." That didn't strike me as being helpful, although I think there may be pastors here who would like to fill me in.

I said to him, "What about goats?" He thought about that one a minute and said, "Well, goats are kind of stubborn, self-willed animals."

Maybe sheep get the praise because they're soft, pliable. At any rate, at that time in my life I thought about this judgment. The Bible says it's the judgment of the nations. I tried to picture it in my mind. It seemed to me it would be a lot like the crowds that gathered at Macy's department store before Christmas, a crowd of people jostling one another.

I could imagine Jesus and some angels coming out on the balcony, and one of the angels would put this harp down and he's picked up a trumpet, and he'd make a noise as they do before a horse race. Everybody would come to attention, and one of the angels would say, "This is the judgment of the sheep and goats. All of you who are sheep go over to the king's right, your left. All of the goats over to the king's left, your right."

Since I had been going to Sunday school, I knew it would be an easy task for us. We'd saunter over to the king's right. My difficulty was with the guys in my gang who didn't go to Sunday school. All of this would be news to them. They didn't know about the judgments. (They regularly consigned one another to hell, but I don't think they really thought it would come about.) I imagined an angel going to Carl Bricalli, Marty Lippin, or Fred Bondieti and trying to explain to them what this is all about.

The angel would say, "You fellows are goats. You're over to the king's left." They'd say, "What do you mean we're goats?" "You're goats." "How come we're goats?" "Well, the king was hungry, and you didn't give him anything to eat. He was thirsty; you didn't give him anything to drink. He was a stranger; you didn't take him in. He needed clothes; you didn't give him any clothes. He was sick; you didn't take care of him. He was in prison; you didn't go to visit him."

They would say, "You've got to be kidding. We never saw him. We never did that."

The angel would explain that there were those who belonged to him, and you didn't help them. I can imagine Andy Madena saying, "Wait a minute. You got to know our neighborhood. You don't take in strangers. Man, next thing you know they're going to mug you. You don't hang around with sick people. You can catch their disease."

No, I just felt it was going to be a fairly tough assignment for whatever angel had to explain that to the guys in my gang.

I came back to this passage recently. I discovered something so obvious I had missed it. Not only do the goats ask the question, "How come we're goats?" the sheep ask the question. The sheep ask, "When was it that we saw you hungry and gave you food, or thirsty and gave you something to drink? And when was it that we saw you a stranger and welcomed you, or naked and gave you clothing? And when was it that we saw you sick or in prison and visited you?"

The sheep are as confused as the goats. I got to thinking about that. It seems to me the basis of that judgment is going to depend on the little unknown, unremembered acts of kindness and love that we hardly think about but are important to the king.

Let me tell you what this isn't saying. This passage isn't saying if you take some change and put it into the box for charity at the checkout counter that by the time the coins hit the bottom you're sure of going to heaven. It's not saying if you put some money in the Salvation Army kettle or if you contribute to somebody's Thanksgiving dinner that demonstrates you belong to Christ.

When the king addresses these that are called sheep, he says, "Come, you who are blessed of my Father and inherit the kingdom that was prepared for you before the creation of the world." That phrase "blessed of my Father" is not a throwaway line. Earlier in the Gospel of Matthew in what is called the Sermon on the Mount, that sermon begins by saying, "Blessed are the poor in spirit, for theirs is the kingdom of heaven." Blessed are the women, the men, who sense a desperate need and have no way in the world to meet the need that they have of God.

And then it says, "Blessed are those who mourn, for they will be comforted." Mourn about what? Mourn about their brokenness, their bankrupt spirit.

And then it says, "Blessed are the meek, for they will inherit the earth." The term 'meek' has the idea of being in submission to God, bowing before him.

The next beatitude says, "Blessed are those who hunger and thirst for righteousness, for they will be filled." There is no such thing as righteousness as though it were something in a box up in heaven. When the Bible talks about righteousness, it is always talking about right relationships—right relationship with God, right relationships with other people. Those who have a brokenness of spirit, who mourn for that brokenness, then begin to crave a relationship with God. That craving is filled as they bow before God. And they also crave a right relationship with others.

The next beatitude says, "Blessed are the merciful, for they will receive mercy." That craving and filling shows itself in mercy.

"Blessed are the pure in heart, for they will see God." God has done something in their innermost being.

"Blessed are the peacemakers, for they will be called children of God."

Matthew 25 says that those who belong to this king, who have allowed him to do a work deep in their lives, are characterized by little unremembered acts of kindness and love that flow from their inner nature—which has been touched by God—as naturally as wool comes from the back of a sheep.

I thought about that. I tried to picture that judgment, and I tried to picture myself as I stood before that king. The king says to me, "Robinson, did you bring your date book?"

I say, "Well, yes, Lord. I know they said I couldn't take anything with me, but I managed to get it through. I've got it right here."

The king says, "Look up March 6, 1996."

"Oh yes, I remember that, Lord. That's when *Newsweek* said I was one of the better communicators in the English-speaking world. I remember that."

The king says, "Well, I never read the newsmagazines. You know how inaccurate they are, that they would say something like that about you."

The king might say, "Do you remember after class on that day? You were headed for another appointment, and there was a young woman sitting at the back of the class. She just sat there when everyone left, and you stopped and talked to her. She said her father had died, and the month before her brother had died. And you sat and talked to her. Do you remember that?"

"I guess so, Lord."

The king will say, "I remember it. When you stopped to talk to that young woman, you were talking to me.

"Look up November 17, 1984."

"Oh yes. I remember that, Lord. That's when I was the president of the Evangelical Theological Society. I remember reading a paper on the relationship of hermeneutics to homiletics."

The king will say, "Well, I never attended many of those meetings. I found them a little stuffy myself. I read the title of your paper, and I didn't understand it. No, do you remember that morning your wife, Bonnie, told you about a couple at the seminary that was having a hard time financially? They didn't know how they would make it through the month, and you took some money and put it in an envelope and dropped it in their box?"

"I don't know if I remember that."

And the king will say, "I remember it. What you gave to that young couple you gave to me, and I've never forgotten it."

When we come to that last judgment, there are going to be all kinds of surprises. There are going to be folks there who are absolutely certain that they are sheep. They're ready to saunter over to the king's right-hand side, and he'll stop them. And they'll say, "Of course we qualify. We have prophesied in your name. We've done miracles in your name. We climbed to the top of the ecclesiastical ladder." And the king will say, "You're goats in sheep's clothing. I never knew you."

And then there will be other people who have been broken by their sinfulness, ashamed of things in their lives, who will wonder if there's even a ghost of a chance that they'll get into that kingdom. They'll conclude that the only possibility is for them to rely on the grace and the favor and the kindness of God in providing some way for them to come. But they'll look at themselves and wonder if they're going to make it in. And they *will* make it, in brokenness of spirit, throwing themselves on God's grace.

A lot of surprises at the judgment.

You men and women, this is a great night. I hope you enjoy it. You'll get a diploma. They'll even give you the tassel that you have on your hat. I hope you'll put it up in your office and from time to time look at it. It says something about what you've accomplished. But when you come to that judgment, I wouldn't bring it with you, because in that day what will matter is not whether you've got a degree from a seminary. What will matter is not that folks applaud you. What will matter is whether in the depths of your life you have allowed God's Spirit to work, and there have come from your inner life acts of kindness and love that you didn't think much about at all but they been ministry to the king.

There are going to be a lot of surprises at that judgment. A lot of surprises.

Haddon Robinson is Harold John Ockenga Distinguished Professor of Preaching at Gordon-Conwell Theological Seminary, in South Hamilton, Massachusetts, and author of Biblical Preaching.

Chapter 9

Imaginative Preaching

The event of preaching is an event in transformed imagination.

Walter Brueggemann[1]

Introduction

*W*alter Burghardt once asked, "What has imagination to do with preaching?" and answered, "Not much, just everything."[2] Garrett Green would agree and add that imagination is even the "divine-human point of contact." He writes, "Proclamation . . . can be described as an appeal to the imagination of the hearers through the images of scripture. The preacher's task is to mediate and facilitate that encounter by engaging his or her own imagination, which becomes the link between scripture and congregation."[3]

In other words, according to Green, what links together the various facets of preaching—the preacher, the exegesis of the text, sermon writing, and the congregation—is our imagination. "Imagination is the meeting place of God and humankind," affirms Barbara Brown Taylor, "the chamber between heaven and earth where the sacred and commonplace mingle and flow in unexpected ways."[4]

In this chapter we will examine five ways to understand the relationship between imagination and proclamation. James Loder, for example, points us to the work of the Holy Spirit; Paul Scott Wilson suggests imagination is a function of language; Fred Craddock invites us to use our imagination to understand our particular community; Walter Brueggemann offers that imagination can help us "reimagine" our lives in light of the gospel; and Barbara Brown Taylor guides us towards the concept of imagination as risk.

James Loder: The Holy Spirit and Preaching

For the past twenty-five years Rudolf Bohren has maintained that the central act of sermon preparation is opening ourselves to the leading of the Holy Spirit.[5] Historically, however, most homileticians have approached the role of the Holy Spirit in preaching cautiously, fearing an overreliance might replace scholarship and exegesis. Fred Craddock, for example, warns that, "Any work of the Holy Spirit which relieves me of my work and responsibility is plainly false."[6] But most do agree that it is the Holy Spirit which illuminates the text, not the preacher. Thomas Long has said, "In preaching, creativity has little to do with inventiveness and everything to do with faithfulness to what the Spirit creates through the text."[7]

Bohren suggests therefore that the preacher invite the Holy Spirit to participate in every aspect of sermon preparation. A model of such an intentional invitation is found in the work of James Loder, who maintains that we can connect with the Holy Sprit *through our human spirit*. His process involves four steps.

The first step he calls *conflict in context*. This tension occurs when we acknowledge and more importantly welcome the stops and starts of preparing a sermon. In Loder's paradigm, this conflict can prompt an *interlude for scanning*—moments when we daydream, stand in front of a shelf of commentaries, rub our eyes. Loder believes this act of scanning opens our human spirit—our insight, our imagination—to the Holy Spirit. If we intentionally open ourselves to the Spirit during such moments, then we are more likely to have a *constructive act of the imagination*—a moment when a detail is revealed in the text, a pertinent newspaper article comes to mind.

After the *release of energy* that occurs when our imagination has been met by the Holy Spirit, the final step is *verifying* what we believe the Spirit has brought to our attention. We might ask as Jonathan Edwards once did, "[Does this work] raise esteem for Jesus, produce a greater regard for the scriptures . . . produce a longing for God and Christ, preach peace and good will, inspire kindness and produce delight in the children of God?"[8]

Loder's model engages our imagination by framing it in the context of the Holy Spirit working as Jesus Christ promised, as "teacher" and "guide." If we intentionally open our human spirit to the Holy Spirit, says Loder, the Spirit will speak through our imagination and guide us in our sermon preparation.[9]

Paul Scott Wilson: The Imagination of the Heart

While Loder suggests how the Holy Spirit might work together with our imagination, Paul Scott Wilson interprets imagination as a function of language to be nurtured and developed. He writes that "The preacher's imagination is leavened by both experience and the Scriptures."[10] In particular, imagination is leavened when scripture, our lives, and the life of a congregation intersect. Wilson writes, "Imagination of the heart . . . We may understand it as the *bringing together of two ideas that might not otherwise be connected and developing the creative energy they generate. . . .* Imagination is released by an ability to use polarities in language to create fresh ideas."[11]

Wilson suggests we explore "four key and universal polarities in the preaching task: biblical text and our situation; law and gospel (or judgment and grace); story and doctrine; and finally, pastor and prophet."[12] In Wilson's model, we introduce two such polarities that share little in common and watch for sparks. For example, Wilson takes the word "salvation" and suggests if we pair it with something unexpected such as "salvation is eating a meal," new connections and associations emerge. The point, writes Wilson, is to search for connections that "open fresh and yet familiar biblical horizons of faith."[13]

The key to Wilson's method is cultivating what R.E.C. Browne called an "untidiness of mind," an untidiness that grants the imagination sufficient time to roam and locate such polarities.[14] Taylor writes,

> When imagination comes home and empties its pocket, of course there will be some sorting to do. Keep the cat's-eye marble, the Japanese beetle wing, the red feather, the penny. Jettison the bottle cap, the broken glass, the melted chocolate stuck with lint. But do not scold imagination from bringing it all home or for collecting it in the first place. There are no treasures without some trash, and the Holy Spirit can be trusted to go with us . . . and to lead us back home again, with eyes far wiser for all they have seen.[15]

Wilson's charge is we locate and introduce poles of language that create fresh "metaphors for faith."[16] Some we may discard, others file away, but in the pile, in the midst of the "untidiness," will arise a spark, a word of truth, a word to be preached.

Fred Craddock: The Empathetic Imagination

Fred Craddock's understanding of the work of the imagination in preaching swivels the spotlight from the preacher's study to imagination's role in enabling a preacher to better understand those in the congregation. He calls such imagination "empathetic."

We discover and engage our "empathetic imagination," suggests Craddock, when we intentionally assemble information about our congregation—by reading the local newspaper, sharing a cup of coffee with the chief of police. We spend time at the Little League field, in the hospital waiting room, and watch for images that are central to our community. In other words, an empathetic imagination scouts for and then shapes such images into a sermon. Frederick Buechner adds that it is the preacher's charge "to hold up life for us, by whatever gifts he or she has of imagination, eloquence, simple candor, to create images of life through which we can somehow see into the wordless truth of our lives."[17] To engage our empathetic imagination, Craddock offers the following exercise:

> Take a blank sheet of paper and write at the top, 'What It's Like to Be?' Beneath that write a phrase descriptive of one concrete facet of human experience. Examples might be: "facing surgery," "living alone," "suddenly wealthy," "rejected by a sorority," "fired from one's position," "fourteen years old." [Then] for the next fifteen minutes scribble on the page every thought, recollection, feeling, experience, name, place, sound, smell, or taste that comes to mind.[18]

This exercise will produce four results.

1) We will soon preach "*for* and not *at* our congregation."
2) It will reveal "how much understanding of the human condition has not been adequately reflected in either the words or music of [our] preaching."[19]
3) We will "reap a harvest of ideas."
4) And finally, we will experience a "noticeable reduction in the number of sermons that make no contact with the listener."[20]

Walter Brueggemann: Preaching as Reimagining

While imagination can assist us in sifting for images that describe the life of our congregation, Walter Brueggemann believes it also enables the preacher to offer images of faithful discipleship. He writes in his book *Cadences of Home* that "the work of preaching is an act of imagination . . . that is, the reimagination of reality according to the evangelical script of the Bible."[21] In other words, imagination can offer images that suggest new ways to treat a spouse, work with a colleague, allocate time, pray, read scripture. Barbara Brown Taylor believes this particular work of the imagination is critical. She writes, "The church's central task is an imaginative one. By that I do not mean a fanciful or fictional task, but one in which the human capacity to imagine—to form mental pictures of the self, the neighbor, the world, the future, to envision new realities—is both engaged and transformed.[22] The preacher has the opportunity to offer images that reveal and celebrate the broad life of the church. She might say, "Look over here at this prayer circle celebrating its thirtieth anniversary. Has anyone spoken to the youth about their mission trip to Washington, D.C.? Have you noticed how our homeless meal has transformed our attitude towards mental illness?" If we carry these images into the pulpit, our congregation can begin to reimagine their lives with the same gospel vision.

Barbara Brown Taylor: Imagination as Risk

When asked what advice she would give a preacher, Barbara Brown Taylor said,

> That's easy. Increase your life. Live your life more fully. And pay attention to it. . . . Stay as alive as you dare, and trust that your life with all its unorthodox twists and turns is still God's territory. Dare to tell some stories that don't sound like religious stories. Use some language that doesn't sound like it belongs in church. Read fiction. Take clogging lessons. Go be alive, so that you yourself are a living sermon about abundant life. Then whatever you say will be worth listening to.[23]

In order to preach well, suggests Taylor, we must take risks: with life, an exegetical style, a sermon structure. If we let imagination push us into unfamiliar places—a high ropes course, a first-person sermon—our preaching will come alive.

We all, of course, fret about failure, physical harm, looking foolish. Insecurity often paralyzes us and we set aside for another week introducing poles of language, working through empathetic exercises, imagining a new reality for ourselves and our congregation. But understanding imagination as an invitation to risk means emptying our bag of sermonic tools and approaching the next sermon as if it were our very first. Offer a conclusion as a celebration, as Henry Mitchell suggests. Hammer out a sermon structure that resembles Eugene Lowry's homiletical plot. Take clogging lessons, skydive, and share how it feels. Natalie Goldberg writes, "Push yourself beyond when you think you are done with what you have to say. Go a little further. Sometimes when you think you are done, it is just the edge of beginning. Probably that's why we decide we're done. It's getting too scary. We are touching onto something real."[24]

The act of climbing into the pulpit has been described by James Earl Massey as a "burdensome joy." When we allow imagination to push us towards new frontiers, that push is often felt as a burden and a joy. But remember when our steps are uncertain, our words hesitant, God is often the closest; for it is then we are no longer depending on our wits, our seminary professors, or treasured preaching books, but on grace, and God's promise if we risk, like Isaiah, raising what might appear as a hot coal to our lips, the word of God will be proclaimed.

SERMONS

"ultima Thule"

Michael Lindvall   Genesis 12:1–9

I don't have a sermon as such for you this week, but I have a letter I'd like to read to you. It's from a minister friend of mine named David Battles. He writes once and again and favored me with another letter this last week. He is, as some of you may know, the pastor of a little Presbyterian church in North Haven, Minnesota, a town of about a thousand—fewer every year—in the rich grassland southwest of the Minnesota River.

Dear Michael,
   Never underestimate the danger hidden in the pages of books. Lamont Wilcox read books, every one of C.S. Forester's Horatio Hornblower novels—epic sea adventures set in the Napoleonic Wars. Lamont read these stories and retreated to the barn to build a boat. He drank too much, neglected the farm, and finally sailed off to the Caribbean without his wife, Annette, who didn't want to go anyway. All this because his high school English teacher, the late Miss Pratt, had given him her old Book-of-the-Month-Club copy of *Captain Hornblower in the Caribbean*.
   My daughter, Jennifer, who just turned eighteen and graduated from high school this past month, also reads books, and what she read in her books got her—and me—into trouble of sorts. She took to reading, of all things, the classics—in translation, of course—as well as popular histories of the Greeks and the Romans. The ancients have fascinated her ever since a sixth-grade field trip to the University of Minnesota Museum where she beheld what she soberly described to her mother and me upon her return that night as "very, very old things." In the reading that followed, she stumbled across a mysterious phrase, half Latin, half Greek, that has puzzled scholars for centuries, two words that came to fascinate my daughter. The ancients, she learned, believed in a place named "ultima Thule." They spoke of it and believed it existed, though they are not of one mind about precisely where ultima Thule may be. They were in agree-

ment only on one point, that ultima Thule was the northernmost land where people lived. Some historians have guessed that it was Norway, others the Shetland Islands or perhaps even Iceland. Wherever ultima Thule lay, a spiritual mist enshrouded the very words; ultima Thule was the end of the earth, the last place one could go, the ultimate destination. These last years, my daughter has discovered boys, the relationship between grades and getting into college, the inspiring tedium of working in the A&W Drive-In, and the anxiety provoked by letters arriving from the colleges to which she applied. Through all of these adolescent vagaries, ultima Thule has stood, it seems, for a sanctuary in her adolescent soul—the place apart, the great destination, the journey's end.

Her daily bus rides to high school in Sleepy Eye that began four years ago have been a repeated emblem to her mother and me, and I think to Jennifer herself, of her growing up and leaving us. Each day's journey to Sleepy Eye carried her closer to the day she would leave home for good. This is a prospect that every parent of a teenager greets with wildly mixed emotions. Annie said this spring that the only thing worse than Jennifer leaving home in the fall would be Jennifer staying home in the fall. When those bus rides began and continued into that first freshman winter, the big orange thing rumbling away in the dark of the morning and the brakes squeaking to announce her return in the dark of the late afternoon, my daughter and I made an emotional lunge for each other, knowing the real parting that was coming in four years. We were not then ready for it in the way we are now, and in the moment we made a rash promise. We promised each other that after high school, father and daughter would take a trip together, a very special trip. The making of that promise fell on the dark early December morning of an impending snowstorm. But the buses were running anyway. We were at breakfast, I was playing with my oatmeal and casting glances out the window every thirty seconds to look for snow, and then back at my daughter, growing up too fast, unafraid of the slippery roads between North Haven and Sleepy Eye, but suddenly aware that everything was on the cusp of changing forever. "When you graduate, Sweets, let's take a trip, just you and me, a father-and-daughter trip."

"Could we, I mean really?"

"You betcha. Where should we go?"

Her answer was unreflective and immediate: "Let's go to ultima Thule." I remember looking at my oatmeal, then out the window to see the first snowflakes in the morning darkness, and saying, "Well, sure." Daughters have this way with fathers, my wife says. Anyway, it was four years away, and nobody knows where ultima Thule is.

The great trip was lost in the litter of high school, forgotten, or so I thought, until the day the acceptance letter came from St. Olaf's College. The letter said that freshman were to report for orientation on Wednesday, the twenty-eighth of August. Jennifer read the letter aloud to us, accented that date, looked thoughtfully at me and said, "Dad, that means the trip will have to be the middle of July. That's the only time Doris will let me off from the A&W." With that she left the room to start phoning friends. Annie looked at me and asked, "What trip?" "The trip to ultima Thule," I said. "Where?" my patient wife asked.

High school seniors, for all their fresh wisdom, have only the loosest grip on geographic and financial realities. When I outlined to my daughter the tuition, room and board costs at St. Olaf, and then estimated costs of getting to even the most accessible of the possible locations of ultima Thule, she looked at the numbers in the same way that I might look at the Pentagon budget: the numerical imagination of mortals can scarcely ascend to such heights. I frankly thought that both ultima Thule and a trip with her father would have shed some of the intrigue they had earlier held, but not so. Ultima Thule had become a necessary punctuation mark for my daughter in her imagined passage from childhood to adulthood. As her spirit matured in the years since she first asked to go there, ultima Thule had become something more. It was no mere spot on a map, but that point of greatest inaccessibility, perhaps the greatest point of spiritual inaccessibility, that deep and far place where hidden things might be seen.

So I got out a map, not a map of the world, not a map of the U.S., but a map of Minnesota. I unfolded it between us on the kitchen table next to the yellow notepad on which tuition numbers lay next to estimated airfare for two to Norway. I smoothed its folds and pointed to North Haven near the bottom. Then I pulled my finger toward me, north, straight and slowly north, past Willmar, past Sauk Centre, past Park Rapids and Bemiji, north across the two Red Lakes, north to the Lake of the Woods, and finally across that huge lake to a little nook of land surrounded by the water and attached only to Manitoba. "The Northwest Angle," I said, "the ultima Thule of Minnesota. The only ultima Thule your old man can afford."

Minnesota's Northwest Angle is maybe the most notorious error in the history of modern surveying. The border between the eastern half of the U.S. and Canada is formed by water: the St. Lawrence River, then four of the Great Lakes, and finally between northeastern Minnesota and Ontario, by the Pigeon and the Rainy Rivers. The Rainy flows into the Lake of the Woods, and there the border jogs oddly northward across that cold water to the point where it was supposed to meet the U. S.-Canadian border coming from the west, that twelve-hundred-mile line drawn straight with a ruler east from the Pacific Ocean. But somebody made a mistake—a twenty-five-mile mistake: the borders didn't meet. They stranded a little hunk of Minnesota in the Lake of the Woods, one hundred square miles of land surrounded on three sides by lake, all of it jutting north above the international border like the valve sticking out of the top of an old pressure cooker.

Such a tale of historical accident and the obvious remoteness of the place made it an ultima Thule nearly as satisfactory to an eighteen-year-old as the Shetland Islands—and one to which you could drive. I learned when I called for a cabin at Angle Inlet, where the road ends and the only place in the Angle with a name, that it was just twenty-some years ago that they built the road. "Used to be you had to get Faye to bring ya' over from Warroad in his diesel boat," said Arne as he took my reservation. I was late to be calling, he said. The cabin was probably the last available anytime in July anywhere in the Angle. And I could only get the last cabin for three days in the middle of the week. Long enough, I thought, in ultima Thule.

That my eighteen-year-old deigned to take a road trip with her father was a wonder to all who heard of it. But children, for all of their rumored spontaneity, are also lovers of routine and predictability. This trip had been a landmark in Jennifer's mental landscape for all the years I had forgotten I had made the offer. Her anticipation made her a garrulous traveling companion. We left right after church, skipping Annie's offer of lunch, eager to be on the way to ultima Thule. In the space of fifty miles, the front seat of the Taurus became something of a confessional booth. Away from the strictures of familiarity, Jennifer talked and talked, inspired to transparency (as we all often are) by the increasing proximity of what one has so eagerly awaited. Jennifer talked about her friends, about college, what would she major in, what would her roommate from Edina be like. And for my benefit, I would guess, she allowed as to how she'd miss her family, "but I'll be home some weekends, you know." As she said the words, I recalled making that same hollow promise in all earnestness a mere thirty years ago. The drive is two-lane highway all the way, Minnesota 71 due north most of the way. The miles and the words rolled on as open farmland yielded to stands of birch and pine, and then into the big woods that stretch to Hudson Bay.

We stopped for the night in Bemiji. After dinner I took Jennifer's picture with the awful statue of Paul Bunyan that you see on all the postcards. She's a big girl, but looked tiny next to Paul. Next morning found Jennifer—and even her father—as full of expectation as seven-year-olds on Christmas Eve. Jennifer drove—too fast, I kept telling her, for the road that skirted the west shore of Red Lake. The woods that flashed by on either side of the car were now unbroken, dark and impenetrable to the eye on that cool and overcast Monday. Not far beyond Warroad you cross the border into Manitoba. The blacktop gives way to gravel, mile upon mile of gravel sliced through the woods, and then a sign, a sign proclaiming that long-ago surveyors' mistake: "Welcome to the United States of America." We arrived in Angle Inlet tired, the heater dial on the Taurus well into the red zone. As Arne showed us to our cabin it began to rain. He cast us a sideways glance and said, "Hope it don't turn to snow." The cabin was small, illuminated by two bizarre, ultramodern fixtures hanging from bare wires, clearly design fancies of the sixties. Arne pointed at the fireplace and said kindling and firewood were out back, was there anything else we needed?

The kindling and the firewood and the newspaper were damp, everything was damp. Starting a fire was a comedy of errors. The heavy, wet air in the fireplace was loath to draw, the damp kindling smoked. Jennifer and I were in our hooded sweatshirts pulled tight around our faces, both of us kneeling before the fire and blowing on the kindling. We blew until I started to feel light-headed and she started to giggle. We laughed, laughed at the scene, laughed about cold and damp ultima Thule, laughed until the fire smoked and went out. We ate Fritos and bean dip, put on all our clothes, took our sleeping bags and went to bed, me on the couch in front of the fire that wasn't, and Jennifer in the only bed.

I awoke with the sleeping bag pulled around my ears, but cold nevertheless. I looked into the first moment of wakefulness to see my daughter sitting at the table. She was drinking Coke from a can and had a map spread out before her. She was crying. I crawled out of the warmth into the very cold air of the cabin. On this July morning, the temperature in our ultima Thule had fallen to the upper thirties. I sat down across from her. "Disappointed?" She nodded and dried her face with the sleeve of her new St. Olaf sweatshirt. "I went for a walk just now," she said. "It looks like all the other woods we drove through. And it's cold, and Arne says the only reason people come here is to fish. I hate to fish."

"You want to go home?" I asked. I glanced at the map between us on the table. She shook her head, and composed herself, looking at me like she does whenever she is getting ready to say something that she has been thinking about. "Dad, it's not the being here, you know, it's actually the going that really matters. I mean, the best part of this whole trip was thinking about it all through high school, and the drive was just as good, and stopping to see Paul Bunyan. Maybe the best part was trying to start the fire last night and blowing on the kindling together and the smoke all over the cabin and then laughing so hard. I felt like that when I graduated last month. Graduation itself wasn't much, it was the getting there. But graduation wasn't an end. Next month I move to Northfield for college, and then I'll graduate in four years, and then I'll probably go to work. Maybe I'll get married and then maybe have kids. But, none of those things is ever it, none of them are, like, the end. You don't ever arrive, Dad, there is no ultima Thule. It's the getting there, it's the trip itself that's the thing."

"So you ready to head home?" I asked. She looked down at the map, which was, I noticed for the first time, not a map of Minnesota, but of Manitoba. She pointed to a spot over on my side of the table, north, far north, the place where the roads ended and the tundra began. "How long would it take us to get to Flin Flon?" she asked. "Days," I said, "days of driving." "Good," she said, "let's go."

We talked, but not as much. Jennifer slept for hundreds of miles on end and I remembered her words over the map. They were familiar words of wisdom. I knew I had heard or read something like them before. It was, I remembered on the way home, Luther, of all people. I remembered just south of Wadena. I looked them up when I got home and typed them out and put them in an envelope, an envelope that Jennifer will find in the care package we are putting together for the first month at college. What Luther said was this: "This life, therefore, is . . . not being, but becoming, not rest but exercise. We are not yet what we shall be, but we are growing toward it; the process is not yet finished, but is going on; this is not the end, but it is the road."

Your friend, Dave.

Michael Lindvall is the senior pastor at First Presbyterian Church, Ann Arbor, Michigan. He is the author of The Good News from North Haven.

"God's Daring Plan"

Barbara Brown Taylor   Luke 2:8–9

Once upon a time—or before time, actually, before there were clocks or calendars or Christmas trees—God was all there was. No one knows anything about that time because no one was there to know it, but somewhere in the middle of that time before time, God decided to make a world. Maybe God was bored or maybe God was lonely or maybe God just liked to make things and thought it was time to try something big.

Whatever the reason, God made a world—this world—and filled it with the most astonishing things: with humpback whales that sing and white-striped skunks that stink and birds with more colors on them than a box of Crayola crayons. The list is way too long to go into here, but suffice it to say that at the end when God stood back and looked at it all, God was pleased. Only something was missing. God could not think what it was at first, but slowly it dawned on him.

Everything he had made was interesting and gorgeous and it all fit together really well, only there was nothing in the world that looked like him, exactly. It was as if he had painted this huge masterpiece and then forgotten to sign it, so he got busy making his signature piece, something made in his own image, so that anyone who looked at it would know who the artist was.

He had one single thing in mind at first, but as he worked God realized that one thing all by itself was not the kind of statement he wanted to make. He knew what it was like to be alone, and now that he had made a world he knew what it was like to have company, and company was definitely better. So God decided to make two things instead of one, which were alike but different, and both would be reflections of him— a man and a woman who could keep him and each other company.

Flesh was what he made them out of—flesh and blood—a wonderful medium, extremely flexible and warm to the touch. Since God, strictly speaking, was not made out of anything at all, but was pure mind, pure spirit, he was very taken with flesh and blood. Watching his two creatures stretch and yawn, laugh and run, he found to his surprise that he was more than a little envious of them. He had made them, it was true, and he knew how fragile they were but their very breakability made them more touching to him, somehow. It was not long before God found himself falling in love with them. He liked being with them better than

/ 159

any of the other creatures he had made, and he especially liked walking with them in the garden in the cool of the evening.

It almost broke God's heart when they got together behind his back, did the one thing he had asked them not to do and then hid from him— from *him!*—while he searched the garden until way past dark, calling their names over and over again. Things were different after that. God still loved the human creatures best of all, but the attraction was not mutual. Birds were crazy about God, especially ruby-throated hummingbirds. Dolphins and raccoons could not get enough of him, but human beings had other things on their minds. They were busy learning how to make things, grow things, buy things, sell things, and the more they learned to do for themselves, the less they depended on God. Night after night he threw pebbles at their windows, inviting them to go for a walk with him, but they said they were sorry, they were busy.

It was not long before most human beings forgot all about him. They called themselves "self-made" men and women, as if that were a plus and not a minus. They honestly believed they had created themselves, and they liked the result so much that they divided themselves into groups of people who looked, thought, and talked alike. Those who still believed in God drew pictures of him that looked just like them, and that made it easier for them to turn away from the people who were different. You would not believe the trouble this got them into: everything from armed warfare to cities split right down the middle, with one kind of people living on that side of the line and another kind on the other.

God would have put a stop to it all right there, except for one thing. When he had made human beings, he had made them free. That was built into them just like their hearts and brains were, and even God could not take it back without killing them. So God left them free, and it almost killed *him* to see what they were doing to each other.

God shouted to them from the sidelines, using every means he could think of, including floods, famines, messengers, and manna. He got inside people's dreams and if that did not work he woke them up in the middle of the night with his whispering. No matter what he tried, however, he came up against the barriers of flesh and blood. They were made of it and he was not, which made translation difficult. God would say, "Please stop before you destroy yourselves!" But all they could hear was thunder. God would say, "I love you as much now as the day I made you," but all they could hear was a loon calling across the water.

Babies were the exception to this sad state of affairs. While their parents were all but deaf to God's messages, babies did not have any trouble hearing him at all. They were all the time laughing at God's jokes or crying with him when he cried, which went right over their parents' heads. "Colic," the grown-ups would say, or "Isn't she cute? She's laughing at the dust mites in the sunlight." Only she wasn't, of course. She was laughing because God had just told her it was cleaning day in heaven, and that what she saw were fallen stars the angels were shaking from their feather dusters.

Babies did not go to war. They never made hate speeches or littered or refused to play with each other because they belonged to different political parties. They depended on other people for everything necessary to their lives and a phrase like "self-made babies" would have made them laugh until their bellies hurt. While no one asked their opinions about anything that mattered (which would have been a smart thing to do), almost everyone seemed to love them, and that gave God an idea.

Why not create himself as one of these delightful creatures?

He tried the idea out on his cabinet of archangels and at first they were all very quiet. Finally the senior archangel stepped forward to speak for all of them. He told God how much they would worry about him, if he did that. He would be putting himself at the mercy of his creatures, the angel said. People could do anything they wanted to him, and if he seriously meant to become one of them there would be no escape for him if things turned sour. Could he at least create himself as a magical baby with special powers? It would not take much—just the power to become invisible, maybe, or the power to hurl bolts of lightning if the need arose. The baby idea was a stroke of genius, the angel said, it really was, but it lacked adequate safety features.

God thanked the archangels for their concern but said no, he thought he would just be a regular baby. How else could he gain the trust of his creatures? How else could he persuade them that he knew their lives inside and out, unless he lived one like theirs? There was a risk. He knew that. Okay, there was a high risk, but that was part of what he wanted his creatures to know: that he was willing to risk everything to get close to them, in hopes that they might love him again.

It was a daring plan, but once the angels saw that God was dead set on it, they broke into applause—not the uproarious kind but the steady kind that goes on and on when you have witnessed something you know you will never see again.

While they were still clapping, God turned around and left the cabinet chamber, shedding his robes as he went. The angels watched as his midnight-blue mantle fell to the floor, so that all the stars on it collapsed in a heap. Then a strange thing happened. Where the robes had fallen, the floor melted and opened up to reveal a scrubby brown pasture speckled with sheep and— right in the middle of them—a bunch of shepherds sitting around a campfire drinking wine out of a skin. It was hard to say who was more startled, the shepherds or the angels, but as the shepherds looked up at them, the angels pushed their senior member to the edge of the hole. Looking down at the human beings who were all trying to hide behind each other (poor things, no wings), the angel said in as gentle a voice as he could muster, "Do not be afraid; for see—I am bringing you good news of great joy for all the people: to you is born this day in the city of David a savior who is Messiah, the Lord."

And away up the hill, from the direction of town, came the sound of a newborn baby's cry.

Barbara Brown Taylor is an Episcopal priest who has been named one of the most effective preachers in the English-speaking world. Formerly of All Saints' Atlanta and Grace-Calvary, Clarkesville, Georgia, she now holds the Harry R. Butman Chair in Religion and Philosophy at Piedmont College in Demorest, Georgia.

Notes

NOTES TO CHAPTER ONE

1. Edmund Steimle, Morris J. Niedenthal, and Charles L. Rice, *Preaching the Story* (Minneapolis: Fortress, 1983), 12–13.

2. Charles Campbell, *Preaching Jesus* (Eerdmans: Grand Rapids, 1997), 117.

3. John McClure, "Narrative and Preaching: Sorting It All Out," *Journal for Preachers,* Advent 1991, 24–28.

4. Steimle, Niedenthal, and Rice, *Preaching the Story,* 171.

5. Campbell, *Preaching Jesus,* 144.

6. Thomas G. Long, *Preaching and the Literary Forms of the Bible* (Philadelphia: Fortress, 1989), 66–86.

7. Ibid., 74–76.

8. Fred Craddock, *Preaching* (Nashville: Abingdon, 1985), 162.

9. Long, *Preaching and the Literary Forms of the Bible,* 76.

10. Ibid., 77.

11. Ibid., 77–79.

12. Ibid., 79.

13. Ibid., 80–81.

14. Ibid., 80.

15. Ibid., 81–82.

16. Ibid., 81–82.

17. Eugene Lowry, *The Homiletical Plot* (Atlanta: John Knox Press, 1980), 20.

18. Eugene Lowry, *The Sermon* (Nashville: Abingdon Press, 1997), 23–24.

19. Lowry, *The Homiletical Plot,* 76.

20. Ibid., 38.

21. Ibid., 65.

22. Ibid., 66.

23. Ronald Allen, *Patterns of Preaching* (St. Louis: Chalice, 1998), 94.

24. Eugene Lowry, *How to Preach a Parable* (Nashville: Abingdon, 1989), 31.

25. Ibid., 38.

26. Ibid., 38–39.

27. Ibid., 39–40.

28. Ibid., 38–40.

29. Ibid., 173.

30. Fred Craddock, *As One Without Authority* (Enid: Phillips University, 1974), 60.

31. Ibid., 54.

32. Ibid.

33. Ibid.

34. Ibid., 63.

35. Ibid., 65.

36. Thomas G. Long, "Edmund Steimle and the Shape of Contemporary Homiletics," *Princeton Seminary Bulletin* 11 (1990):255.

37. Steimle, *Preaching the Story,* 41.

38. Ibid., 166–67.

39. Ibid., 171.

40. Ibid., 173.

41. Ibid.

42. Campbell, *Preaching Jesus,* 144.

43. David Lose, "Narrative and Proclamation in a Postliberal Homiletic," *Homiletic* Summer 1998, 4.

44. Ibid., 7.

45. Gail O'Day and Thomas G. Long, *Listening to the Word* (Nashville: Abingdon, 1993), 127.

46. W. P. Kinsella, "Joy in Dyersville," US Airways Attaché (July, 1998), 98–99.

NOTES TO CHAPTER TWO

1. Samuel Proctor, *The Certain Sound of the Trumpet* (Valley Forge: Judson Press, 1994), 9.

2. James McBride, *The Color of Water* (New York: Riverhead Books, 1996), 47.

3. James Harris, *Preaching Liberation* (Minneapolis: Fortress Press, 1995), 40–41.

4. Henry Mitchell, *Celebration and the Experience of Preaching* (Nashville: Abingdon, 1990), 69.

5. Henry H. Mitchell, *Black Preaching The Recovery of a Powerful Art* (Nashville: Abingdon, 1990), 122.

6. Mitchell, *Celebration and the Experience of Preaching,* 64.

7. Harris, *Preaching Liberation,* 52–53.

8. Mitchell, *Celebration and the Experience of Preaching,* 89.

9. Mitchell, *Black Preaching,* 63.

10. Mitchell, *Celebration and the Experience of Preaching,* 80.

11. Proctor, *The Certain Sound of the Trumpet,* 19.

12. Ibid., 20.

13. Ibid., 33.

14. Ibid., 41–43.

15. Samuel Proctor, *How Shall They Hear?* (Valley Forge: Judson Press, 1992), 9–10.

16. Proctor, *The Certain Sound of the Trumpet,* 68.

17. Ibid., 95.

18. Ibid.

19. Ibid., 116–18.

20. Mitchell, *Black Preaching,* 39.

21. Ibid.

22. Richard Lischer, *The Preacher King* (New York: Oxford University Press, 1995), 94.

23. Ibid., 97–98.

24. Ibid., 106.

25. Ibid., 110.

26. Ibid., 102.

27. Mitchell, *Celebration,* 140.

28. Samuel G. Freedman, *Upon This Rock: The Miracles of a Black Church* (New York: HarperCollins, 1993), 182.

29. Proctor, *How Shall They Hear,* 99.

30. Harris, *Preaching Liberation,* 3.

31. James Cone, *God of the Oppressed* (San Francisco: Harper & Row, 1975), 82.

32. Ibid., 139.

33. Harris, *Preaching Liberation,* 9.

34. Justo L. and Catherine G. Gonzalez, *The Liberating Pulpit* (Nashville: Abingdon, 1994), 15.

35. Lischer, *Preacher King,* 138.

36. Evans Crawford with Thomas H. Troeger, *The Hum Call and Response in African American Preaching* (Nashville: Abingdon Press, 1995), 13.

37. Ibid., 16.

38. From the hymn "O for a Closer Walk with God."

NOTES TO CHAPTER THREE

1. Annie Dillard, *The Writing Life* (New York: Harper & Row, 1989), 68.

2. Henry Sloane Coffin, *What to Preach* (New York: George H. Doran, 1926), 163.

3. Thomas G. Long and Neely Dixon McCarter, eds., *Preaching In and Out of Season* (Louisville: Westminster/John Knox Press, 1990), 77.

4. William H. Willimon, *The Intrusive Word* (Grand Rapids: Eerdmans, 1994), 1.

5. Ibid., 4.

6. Ibid., 132–33

7. Ibid., 4.

8. Ibid., 61.

9. Ibid., 64.

10. Ibid., 135.

11. Ibid., 104.

12. Ibid., 22.

13. H. Richard Niebuhr, *Christ and Culture* (New York: Harper & Row, 1951), vii.

14. Ibid., 39.

15. Tony Campolo, *Can Mainline Denominations Make a Comeback* (Valley Forge: Judson, 1995), 29.

16. Tony Campolo, *20 Hot Potatoes Christians Are Afraid to Touch* (Dallas: Word, 1988), 72.

17. Campolo, *Can Mainline Denominations Make a Comeback,* 29.

18. Ibid., 46.

19. Ibid., 40.

20. Ibid., 30.

21. Ibid., 30–31.

22. Ibid., 53.

23. Ibid., 64.

24. Ibid., 67.

25. Ibid., 110.

26. Ibid., 85.

27. Ibid., 116.

28. Ibid., 90.

29. Ibid., 48.

30. Ibid., 19.

31. Ibid., 72.

32. Long and McCarter, *Preaching In and Out of Season,* 83.

33. Craig Loscalzo, *Evangelistic Preaching That Connects* (Downers Grove: Intervarsity, 1995), 16.

34. Flannery O'Connor, *The Violent Bear It Away*, in *Collected Works* (New York: Library of America), 437.

35. Quoted by Jurgen Moltmann in *The Spirit of Life,* trans. Margaret Kohl (Minneapolis: Fortress, 1992), 127.

36. Quoted by William Willimon, *Remember Who You Are* (Nashville: Upper Room, 1980), 59.

37. William James, *The Varieties of Religious Experience* (New York: Modern Library, 1902), 169.

38. Elizabeth Dewberry Vaughan, *Break the Heart of Me* (Garden City: Doubleday, 1994), quoted in *The Christian Century,* January 18, 1995.

39. Robert A. Heinlein, *Job: A Comedy of Justice* (New York: Ballantine, 1984), 124.

40. Annie Dillard, *An American Childhood* (New York: Harper, 1987), 195.

41. E. Stanley Jones, "Conversions," quoted in *Devotional Classics,* Richard Foster and James Bryan Smith, eds. (San Francisco: Harper Collins, 1990), 301.

42. Robertson Davies, *The Cunning Man* (New York: Viking, 1994), 434–35.

NOTES TO CHAPTER FOUR

1. John Broadus, *On the Preparation and Delivery of Sermons* (Harper & Brothers, 1944), 50.

2. Henry Emerson Fosdick, *The Living of These Days* (New York: Harper & Brothers, 1956), 92–93.

3. Fred Craddock, *As One Without Authority* (Enid: Phillips University Press, 1971), 18–19.

4. Ronald J. Allen, *Preaching the Topical Sermon* (Louisville: Westminster/John Knox Press, 1992), ix.

5. James Earl Massey, *Designing the Sermon* (Nashville: Abingdon, 1980), 21.

6. Thomas G. Long, *The Witness of Preaching* (Louisville: Westminister/John Knox Press, 1989), 49.

7. Allen, *Preaching the Topical Sermon,* 3.

8. Ibid., 4.

9. Long, *The Witness of Preaching,* 49.

10. Ibid., 5.

11. Allen, *Preaching the Topical Sermon,* 38–39.

12. Ibid., 42–43.

13. Ibid., 54.

14. Ibid., 57.

15. Ibid., 60.

16. Ibid., 62.

17. Ibid., 75.

18. Ibid., 80–81.

19. Ibid., 84.

20. Ibid., 86.

21. Ibid., 89.

22. Ibid., 92.

23. Ibid.. 4.

24. Ibid., 19.

25. Mary Pipher, *The Shelter of Each Other* (New York: G.P. Putnam's Sons, 1996), 10.

26. Mary T. Stimming, "Left Out on Mother's Day: Crucifixion Amnesia," *The Christian Century* (May 7, 1997): 436.

27. John 2:4.

28. Mark 3:35.

29. Ruth 1:16.

30. Stanton L. Jones and Don F. Workman, "Homosexuality: The Behavioral Sciences and the Church," in *Homosexuality and the Church: Both Sides of the Debate,* ed. Jeffrey S. Silker (Louisville: Westminster John Knox Press, 1994), 95.

31. Provocative studies of homosexuality and the Bible include Robin Scroggs, *The New Testament and Homosexuality* (Philadelphia: Fortress Press, 1983); Victor Paul Furnish, *The Moral Teaching of Paul,* rev. ed. (Nashville: Abingdon Press, 1985), 52–83; *Biblical Ethics and Homosexuality: Listening to Scripture,* ed. Robert L. Brawley (Louisville: Westminster John Knox Press, 1996); *Homosexuality and Christian Community,* ed. Choon-Leong Seow (Louisville: Westminster John Knox Press, 1996). Especially insightful is Richard B. Hays, *The Moral Vision of the New Testament: Community, Cross, New Creation. A Contemporary Introduction to New Testament Ethics* (San Francisco: HarperSanFrancisco, 1994), 379–406.

32. John Boswell, *Christianity, Social Tolerance and Homosexuality: Gay People in Western Europe from the Beginning of the Christian Era to the*

Fourteenth Century (Chicago: University of Chicago Press, 1980), 131. For other readings of aspects of the tradition, see Cardinal Joseph Ratzinger, "Letter to the Bishops of the Catholic Church on the Pastoral Care of Homosexual Persons (1986)" in *Homosexuality and the Church,* 39–49, and John J. McNeill, "Homosexuality: Challenging the Church to Grow," in *Homosexuality and the Church,* 49–60.

33. Ibid., 169–206.

34. Ibid., 213–15.

35. Ibid., 265–66.

36. Ibid., 269–331.

37. For reflections on moral reasoning in relationshi to this topic, see Lisa Sowle Cahill, "Homosexuality: A Case Study in Moral Argument," in *Homosexuality and the Church,* 61–75, and James B. Nelson, "Sources for a Body Theology," in *Homosexuality and the Church,* 76–92.

38. For overviews, see Joseph Nicolosi and Ruth Fuller, who contribute separate sections to the discussion of "What Does Science Teach about Human Sexuality?" in *Caught in the Crossfire: Helping Christians Debate Homosexuality* (Nashville: Abingdon Press, 1994), 67–88; Stanton Jones and Don Workman, "Homosexuality: The Behavioral Sciences and the Church," in *Homosexuality in the Church,* 93–115; Chandler Burr, "Homosexuality and Biology," in *Homosexuality in the Church,* 116–36.

39. Simon LeVay and Dean H. Hamer, "Evidence for a Biological Influence in Male Homosexuality," *Scientific American* 270 (1994): 43–57; William Byne, "The Biological Evidence Challenged," *Scientific American* 270 (1994): 58–67.

40. For other considerations of experience in relationship to homosexuality, see Joe Dallas, "Another Option: Christianity and Ego-Dystonic Homosexuality," in *Homosexuality and the Church,* 137–44; Virginia Ramey Mollenkott, "Overcoming Heterosexism—To Benefit Everyone," in *Homosexuality and the Church,* 145–49; Chris Glaser, "The Love that Dare Not Pray Its Name: The Gay and Lesbian Movement in America's Churches," in *Homosexuality and the Church,* 125–29.

41. Clark M. Williamson, *Way of Blessing* (St. Louis: Chalice Press, forthcoming).

42. Ibid.

43. For this way of understanding the gospel, see Ronald J. Allen, *Interpreting the Gospel: An Introduction to Preaching* (St. Louis: Chalice Press, 1998), 83–88; Clark M. Williamson and Ronald J. Allen, *The Teaching Minister* (Louisville: Westminster John Knox Press, 1991), 65–82.

44. H. Richard Niebuhr, *The Purpose of the Church and Its Ministry* (New York: Harper and Brothers Publishers, 1956), 27–47.

NOTES TO CHAPTER FIVE

1. Paul Scott Wilson, *The Four Pages of the Sermon* (Nashville: Abingdon, 1999), 155.

2. Ibid., 20.

3. Ibid., 39.

4. Ibid., 46.

5. Ibid., 48.

6. Ibid., 50.

7. Ibid., 56.

8. Ibid., 78.

9. Ibid., 77.

10. Ibid., 82.

11. Ibid., 107.

12. Ibid., 123.

13. Ibid., 116–17.

14. Ibid., 129.

15. Ibid., 163.

16. Ibid.

17. Ibid., 25.

18. Ibid., 170.

19. Ibid., 200.

20. Ibid., 202.

21. Ibid., 203.

22. Ibid., 220.

23. Ibid., 209.

24. Ibid., 200.

25. Richard Lischer, *Theories of Preaching* (Durham: The Labyrinth Press, 1987), 106.

26. Eugene Lowry, *The Sermon* (Nashville: Abingdon, 1997), 78.

27. Wilson, 120.

28. Barbara Brown Taylor, *Gospel Medicine* (Cambridge: Cowley, 1995), 74.

29. Holly Brides, *A Circle of Prayer* (Wildcat Canyon Press: Berkeley, 1997), 4–5.

30. Ibid., 21–24.

NOTES TO CHAPTER SIX

1. Thomas G. Long, *Preaching and the Literary Forms of the Bible* (Philadelphia: Fortress Press, 1989), 127.

2. Don Wardlow, ed., *Preaching Biblically* (Philadelphia: Westminster, 1983), 29–30.

3. Gail R. O'Day and Thomas G. Long, *Listening to the Word* (Nashville: Abingdon, 1993), 150.

4. Long, *Preaching and the Literary Forms of the Bible,* 24.

5. Ibid., 25.

6. Ibid., 26.

7. Ibid., 30.

8. Ibid.

9. Ibid., 34.

10. Ibid., 23.

11. Alyce McKenzie, *Preaching Proverbs* (Louisville: Westminster John Knox Press, 1996), viii.

12. Long, *Preaching and the Literary Forms of the Bible,* 54.

13. McKenzie, *Preaching Proverbs,* 3.

14. Ibid., 20.

15. Ibid., xv.

16. Ibid., 47.

17. Long, *Preaching and the Literary Forms of the Bible,* 65.

18. McKenzie, *Preaching Proverbs,* 22.

19. Long, *Preaching and the Literary Forms of the Bible,* 61–62.

20. Ibid., 43.

21. Ibid., 47.

22. O'Day and Long, *Listening to the Word,* 156.

23. Ibid., 157.

24. Donald E. Gowan, *Reclaiming the Old Testament for the Christian Pulpit* (T & T Clark: Edinburgh, 1980), 146.

25. Elizabeth Achtemeier, *Preaching from the Old Testament* (Louisville: Westminster/John Knox Press, 1989), 148–49.

26. Ibid., 159.

27. Ibid., 160.

28. Ibid., 138.

29. Long, *Preaching and the Literary Forms of the Bible,* 87.

30. Ibid.

31. Ibid., 96–97.

32. Ibid., 95.

33. Ibid., 97.

34. O'Day & Long, 151.

35. Ibid., 153.

36. Ibid., 153.

37. Charles L. Campbell, *Preaching Jesus* (Grand Rapids: Eerdmans, 1997), 178.

38. Dan Otto Via Jr., *The Parables* (Philadelphia: Fortress Press, 1967), 37.

39. Delivered May 18, 1999, at Rochester College before primarily Church of Christ and Christian Church (Evangelical) male preachers.

40. I am indebted to a source now lost for the connection of this movie to a discussion of point of view.

41. I read the parable as cause of offense, doing the work of a metaphor. I have followed Robert Funk's direction, allowing the listener "to be drawn up into the narrative as the narrative prompts." *Parables and Presence: Forms of the New Testament Tradition* (Philadelphia: Fortress, 1982), especially 29–65.

NOTES TO CHAPTER SEVEN

1. Frederick Buechner interviewed in *Reformed Liturgy & Music,* Spring 1994, 59.

2. Thomas G. Long, *The Witness of Preaching* (Louisville: Westminster/John Knox Press, 1989), 44.

3. Ibid., 31.

4. Henry Emerson Fosdick, *The Living of These Days* (New York: Harper & Brothers, 1956), 97–98.

5. William H. Willimon, *Worship as Pastoral Care* (Nashville: Abingdon, 1979), 215.

6. Kathy Black, *A Healing Homiletic* (Nashville: Abingdon, 1996), 33.

7. Ibid., 35.

8. Ibid., 36.

9. Ibid., 37.

10. Ibid., 186.

11. Ibid., 53.

12. Ibid., 183.

13. Ibid.

14. Ibid, 184.

15. Ibid., 184–85.

16. Ibid., 185.

17. Ibid., 36.

18. Leonora Tubbs Tisdale, *Preaching as Local Theology and Folk Art* (Minneapolis: Fortress, 1997), 60.

19. Ibid., 33.

20. Ibid.

21. Ibid., 62–90.

22. Ibid., 92.

23. Ibid., 99.

24. Ibid., 105.

25. Ibid., 141.

26. Ibid., 46.

27. Christine M. Smith, *Weaving the Sermon* (Louisville: Westminster/John Knox Press, 1989), 17.

28. Ibid., 144.

29. Ibid., 40.

30. Ibid., 57.

31. Carol Noren, *The Women in the Pulpit* (Nashville: Abingdon, 1992), 70.

32. Thomas G. Long and Gail R. O'Day, *Listening to the Word* (Nashville: Abingdon, 1993), 185.

33. Long, *The Witness of Preaching*, 33–35.

34. Robert Coles, *The Mind's Fate* (Boston: Little, Brown and Company, 1995), 114.

35. Fosdick, *The Living of the These Days*, 99.

36. David W. Augsburger, *Helping People Forgive* (Louisville: Westminster/John Knox Press, 1996), 21.

37. Ibid.

38. Hinkle as quoted in Augsburger, *Helping People Forgive*, 22.

39. Dr. James Cone gave this lecture at Princeton Theological Seminary, Princeton, New Jersey, on April 5, 1999.

40. This is a paraphrase from memory.

41. Anne Lamott, *Traveling Mercies: Some Thoughts on Faith* (New York: Pantheon Books, 1999), 128.

42. Ibid., 137.

43. Miroslav Volf, "Difficult, Very Difficult," *The Christian Century* (Jan. 27, 1999), 89.

44. Rev. Art Ross, pastor of the White Memorial Presbyterian Church in Raleigh, N.C., preached this sermon entitled "The Highest Form of Love" at the

church on February 14, 1999. The scripture passages were 1 Corinthians 13:1–3, Luke 10:1–11 and Romans 12:18.

45. Augsburger, *Helping People Forgive,* 16.

NOTES TO CHAPTER EIGHT

1. William Willimon, *Shaped by the Bible* (Nashville: Abingdon, 1990), 86.

2. Leander Keck, *The Bible in the Pulpit* (Nashville: Abingdon, 1978), 106.

3. David L. Bartlett, *Between the Bible and the Church: New Methods for Biblical Preaching* (Nashville: Abingdon, 1999), 11.

4. Donald E. Gowan, *Reclaiming the Old Testament for the Christian Pulpit* (Edinburgh: T&T Clark, 1980), 6.

5. Elizabeth Achtemeier, *Preaching from the Old Testament* (Louisville: Westminster/John Knox Press, 1989), 57.

6. Ronald J. Allen and John C. Holbert, *Holy Root, Holy Branches* (Nashville: Abingdon, 1995), 25–26.

7. Ibid., 78.

8. Fred Craddock, *Preaching* (Nashville: Abingdon, 1989), 131.

9. Ibid., 132.

10. Fred Craddock, *Preaching* (Nashville: Abingdon, 1985), 131–32.

11. Ibid., 132.

12. Walter Brueggemann, *Cadences of Home* (Louisville: Westminster John Knox Press, 1997), 3.

13. Ibid., 4–11.

14. Ibid., 12.

15. James Earl Massey, *Designing the Sermon* (Nashville: Abingdon, 1980), 51–52.

16. Ronald Allen, *Patterns of Preaching* (St. Louis: Chalice Press, 1998), 29.

17. John Stott quoted in John MacArthur, *Rediscovering Expository Preaching* (Dallas: Word, 1992), 58.

18. Ronald J. Allen, *Preaching the Topical Sermon* (Louisville: Westminster/John Knox Press, 1992), 2.

19. William Willimon, *The Intrusive Word* (Grand Rapids: Eerdmans, 1994), 38.

20. John MacArthur, *Rediscovering Expository Preaching* (Dallas: Word, 1992), 340–41.

21. Ibid., xv.

22. Robert L. Thomas, quoted in John MacArthur, *Rediscovering Expository Preaching* (Dallas: Word, 1992), 137, 151.

23. John A. Broadus, *On the Preparation and Delivery of Sermons* (New York: Harper & Brothers, 1944), 145.

24. MacArthur, *Rediscovering Expository Preaching,* 347.

25. Ibid., 342.

26. Ibid., 339.

27. Ibid., 343.

28. Ibid., 121.

29. Robinson, *Biblical Preaching,* 77–78.

30. Ibid., 54–55.

31. Ibid., 21.

32. Ibid., 22–23.

33. Ibid., 149.

34. Ibid., 26.

35. Thomas John Carlisle, *Eve and After: Old Testament Women in Portrait* (Grand Rapids: William B. Eerdmans Publishing Co., 1984), 95.

NOTES TO CHAPTER NINE

1. Walter Brueggemann, as quoted in Eugene Lowry, *The Sermon: Dancing on the Edge of Mystery* (Nashville: Abingdon, 1998), 66.

2. Walter Burghardt, *Preaching: The Art and the Craft* (New York: Paulist, 1987), 22.

3. Ibid., 149.

4. Ibid., 213.

5. Richard Lischer, *Theories of Preaching* (Durham: Labyrinth, 1987), 326–30.

6. Fred Craddock, *Preaching* (Nashville: Abingdon Press, 1988), 30.

7. Thomas G. Long, *Preaching the Literary Forms of the Bible* (Philadelphia: Fortress Press, 1989), 134.

8. Nancy Murphey, "Date for Theology," *Theology in the Age of Scientific Reasoning* (Ithaca: Cornell University Press, 1990), 45.

9. James Loder, *The Transforming Moment* (Colorado Springs: Helmers & Howard, 1989), chapter 4. Loder also describes this process in James Loder & Jim Neidhardt, *The Knight's Move* (Colorado Springs: Helmers & Howard, 1992).

10. Paul Scott Wilson, *Imagination of the Heart* (Nashville: Abingdon Press, 1988), 26.

11. Ibid., 32.

12. Ibid., 249.

13. Ibid., 52.

14. R.E.C. Browne, *The Ministry and the Word* (London: SCM Press, 1958), 71.

15. Barbara Brown Taylor, *The Preaching Life* (Cambridge: Cowley, 1993), 48.

16. Wilson, *Imagination*, 252.

17. Frederick Buechner, as quoted in Eugene Lowry's *The Sermon: Dancing on the Edge of Mystery* (Nashville: Abingdon, 1998), 29.

18. Fred Craddock, *Preaching* (Nashville: Abingdon, 1985), 97.

19. Ibid.

20. Ibid., 98–99.

21. Walter Brueggemann, *Cadences of Home: Preaching Among Exiles* (Louisville: Westminster John Knox Press, 1997), 32–33.

22. Taylor, *Preaching Life*, 39.

23. Taped conversation held with Barbara Brown Taylor in 1997 at the College of Preachers, Washington, D.C.

24. Natalie Goldberg, *Writing Down the Bones* (Boston: Shambhala, 1986), 103.